NO-NONSENSE
MANAGEMENT
TIPS
FOR WOMEN

by Jeannette Reddish Scollard

A WALLABY BOOK
Published by Simon & Schuster, Inc.
New York

Copyright © 1983 by Jeannette Reddish Scollard
All rights reserved
including the right of reproduction
in whole or in part in any form
Published by Wallaby Books
A Division of Simon & Schuster, Inc.
Simon & Schuster Building
1230 Avenue of the Americas
New York, New York 10020

Designed by Stanley S. Drate

WALLABY and colophon are registered trademarks of Simon & Schuster, Inc.

First Wallaby Books printing November 1983

10 9 8 7 6 5 4 3 2 1

Manufactured in the United States of America

Printed and bound by Fairfield Graphics

Library of Congress Cataloging in Publication Data

Scollard, Jeannette Reddish.
  No-nonsense management tips for women.

  "A Wallaby book."
  Includes index.
  1. Women executives. I. Title.
HF5500.2.S39   1983   658.4'09'024042   83-14913
ISBN 0-671-49455-4

For
Gary Scollard

CONTENTS

Acknowledgments

Successful women have managed to break through to the hallowed halls of upper management and senior status, but they do not delude themselves. They know they have a long way to go. They are judged by a sterner standard than are their male counterparts.

Generally, they are reluctant to speak out on the matters with which this book is concerned. Some women agreed to speak to me only if I promised to tell no one, ever. Some women spoke to me only off-the-record. All were circumspect in their interviews. There are many unattributed quotes in this book, all taken from notes of interviews that I conducted. Giving these women anonymity was a price worth paying for their candor.

The following are a few of the accomplished women I admire enormously. They are the role models for the younger generation of women.

Elaine Bond, senior vice president, Chase Manhattan Bank
E. Camron Cooper, treasurer, Atlantic Richfield
Pam Dixon, vice president, MGM
Dr. Dorothy Gregg, executive vice president, Research and
    Forecasts, Inc.
Marian Sulzberger Heiskell, outside director on many
    eminent boards
Elaine Linker, vice president, MMT Sales, Inc.
Doris Mattus-Hurley, president, Haagen-Dazs Franchise,
    Inc.
Sandra Meyer, president, Communications Division,
    American Express
Judith Moncrieff, manager of Research and Production,
    Mobil
Colombe Nicholas, president, Christian Dior New York
Mary Eileen O'Keefe, chairman of the board, International
    Coal
Mary Jane Raphael, vice president, ABC
Adelaide Sink, senior vice president, NCNB National Bank
Isabel Sloane, vice president, Morgan Guaranty Trust

I also want to thank Anne-Marie O'Leary for her invaluable assistance.

March 15, 1983   J.R.S.

Note:

While you may not find it realistic or necessary in your particular situation to follow every suggestion or plan as detailed here, the guidelines within these pages will help you delineate your course of action. Clearly, you cannot, and certainly would not, want to mold every piece of your behavior according to how you think others will perceive you. Something must be kept for yourself. What is most important is that you are completely aware of what that something is, and how it might work against your being perceived as a serious business person. You don't have to be perfect. Yet you will want to consider doing enough of the "right" things often enough to make it easy to be identified as a committed candidate for success.

INTRODUCTION

If you are going to be successful in the corporate world, you have to be excellent at what you do. But that is not enough. You also have to make certain the men around you perceive you as excellent—and as management material. To do this, you have to learn the rules of corporate games and how to signal that you are someone special.

Corporations are dominated by men. For the most part, they regard women as irrelevant. Women are excluded from the "old boy" network. They are not routinely initiated into the mysterious rites of business that exist in every corporation, and because they don't know the rules they make many mistakes.

This book tells you what the rules are. It suggests no-nonsense tips that can make a positive difference in how you are perceived by your male counterparts and superiors. It details how to find acceptance in corporate circles. It tells you where the growth jobs are and how to structure your career.

This book describes how a successful woman gets ahead; how she juggles her complicated life without diluting her image as a dedicated business woman. It reveals how she copes with business entertaining, small talk, presentations, affiliations, the wives of her male peers, and her family. It gives you the lingo and jargon she uses to strengthen her communication skills in her largely male environment. It tells you how she treads the fine line between being perceived as a fragile lady and a tough bitch.

Successful women concern themselves with their image. They pay close attention to how their actions, attitude and demeanor are perceived by the male community. It is not enough to be serious, excellent and committed—they also must be *perceived* as serious, excellent and committed.

The executive woman recognizes that being a woman is the worst thing she has going against her. She is aware of the stereotypical negative attitudes men have about women's ability to function as efficiently as men in the work place. She bends over backward to avoid letting men pigeonhole her. She is aware of male mythology about women.

The successful woman knows that she is perpetually educating the men around her. She is well aware that after having dealt with her, a man will be better equipped to understand the next woman he meets who also does not fit his archaic notions. She avoids being obviously patronizing—although it does feel tedious at times for her to maintain her unruffled patience.

Successful women are successful not only because they are extraordinarily good at what they do, but also because they are undiscourageable. They are realistic, tenacious, strong-willed and completely convinced of their executive worth.

PART ONE

CAREER

MASTER

PLAN

A career should always be approached with a plan. The successful woman in the corporate world sits down with pen in hand and consciously contemplates her total career objectives. She takes care to leave herself the flexibility to move in several directions should different opportunities arise, she never forgets her priorities, and she always remembers that her world is constantly changing. Every few years she has a heart-to-heart talk with herself or a trusted mentor to redefine her goals and prospects.

The successful woman does not deliberately slam doors behind herself or cultivate enemies gratuitously. She moves cautiously, nonetheless taking care to appear decisive. Her insecurities are masked from the view of her peers, and she seems to them to move with deliberate confidence.

Some of today's most successful women are surprised at their success. Tomorrow's top women probably won't be. They aim high and hope for the best. If they make it, they will be gratified. If they fall short of their ambitions, they will know that at least they played the game well and gave it their best.

1 STARTING ON THE FAST TRACK

Although the woman who is currently in top management probably did not have a life career plan, the younger woman who has more recently entered the job market would do well to have clearly defined objectives for herself. A young woman should anticipate a forty-year work experience, divided into four segments.

THE PATH

Early in a woman's career, she might benefit most from a politically oriented job that gives her broad exposure to the business community. The ideal is a job in city government, on the governor's staff or, even better, on the White House staff. The Washington, D. C.-based Bureau of the Budget is another place from which an ambitious young woman can make important contacts. An introduction to the business community from a position of power, or a position assumed to be connected to power, gives a woman valuable exposure to the old boy network of business leaders. Moreover, when she picks a job she considers how it's going to look on her resume twenty years down the road. "A woman can't afford to have less than first-class credentials. She should pick first-class institutions to affiliate with. Early on, money isn't as important as her image," notes a highly ranked woman.

"Use your twenties to develop your professional or functional skills," advises Sandra Meyer, president of the Communications Division of American Express. "Learn to be superb in your twenties. Don't worry about your career."

A woman in her twenties should put forth the extra effort to learn as much as possible. "Volunteer to do anything. Pitch in and don't complain," comments Colombe Nicholas, president of Christian Dior in New York. "Get the job done and move on to the next thing. If an executive sees something to be done she doesn't stop until it's done. If something needs to be typed and it is eight at night and no secretary is around and an executive can type, she types."

In her thirties a woman headed for the top builds a solid reputation for herself, using the skills she acquired in the previous decade. She learns to manage herself and to manage other people. "In your forties you bring it all together," notes American Express's Sandra Meyer, who is in her forties and *has* brought it all together.

After twenty years of work experience, the executive has built her expertise and her reputation. She has learned how to motivate subordinates to perform at their peak level. The woman is now ready to take on more important leadership responsibilities. At this point she has the background to win the confidence of her senior management and to persuade them to give her more authority.

The successful woman manager could now be at a management rank where few women have been before. It could well be a level where she detects psychological resistance to promoting her further, because of her gender. She uses her political sensibilities to determine if there is a desirable job in her company that is likely to be open to her. If there is not, she looks around at other companies. She finds one where the management is willing to give a seasoned woman manager the responsibilities she has prepared for.

A woman executive's peak productive years are from forty-five to fifty-five years of age. By the time she reaches fifty, she begins to shift her role to permit the active nurturing and grooming of younger staff members in preparation for turning over her job years hence.

A woman can expect to reach a position close to the apex of her career when she is in her late fifties. At this point, she begins to teach more than to learn. She spends fewer and fewer hours at her office and more time as a chief adviser on boards of directors and at the top level of her own company. Her thirty years of work experience have provided her with a wealth of information that she shares freely.

She may opt not to retire completely, but may remain active by lecturing and counseling the younger generation.

EDUCATION

The woman who is an executive today and is over forty years old probably did not plan her career as carefully as the younger generation of women, who are more realistic about working the rest of their lives. Today's executive woman probably has only a bachelor of arts degree. She started off with low career goals and little dreamed of her current success.

Remarks Colombe Nicholas, who earned a law degree: "I'd recommend to anyone to get as much education as you can. A simple college degree is not enough if you want to be chairman and president of a big corporation. Get both an M.B.A. and a law degree. Or become a C.P.A. Do something in school to show that you have a willingness to go the extra mile. Get additional expertise just to show you're serious."

The woman who is at the top now believes the world has changed too much for a liberal arts major to have a real shot at her job. "Things are different today," notes a New York banking executive. "Don't expect to get away with winging it anymore. You can't afford to have less than top credentials. The ambitious young man has them. The woman is going to have the best background available or she will lose out. Tokenism is passé in the eighties."

A degree in corporate law is also recommended as an excellent background. And women with advanced engineering degrees are finding great demand for their skills.

In today's increasingly computerized offices, the woman who is adept in adapting computers to commonplace business routines may find herself with an added advantage. Computers are being used increasingly in budgeting and money management to do routine tasks.

M.B.A. VERSUS NO M.B.A.

For women as well as for men, the jury is out on whether a masters degree in business administration is a key to corporate success. One thing is certain: It does no harm to anyone's career. The only question is how much benefit it brings.

An M.B.A. certainly has one definite added advantage for women: It makes them look serious about their careers. It marks them as dedicated, smart and hardworking. It offsets the silly notion of women being office amateurs. An M.B.A. says its holder is competitive, highly trained and ready to go.

Moreover, in today's tough economic environment the woman with an M.B.A. is much more likely to find a well-paying "career-beginning" job upon graduation than the woman who has only a liberal arts degree. The graduates from Harvard, Wharton and Stanford have the greatest advantage, since these schools are held in particularly high esteem across the nation. However, an advanced degree from any accredited university is a decided initial advantage. Further, any woman with an M.B.A. is likely to enter the work arena with a substantial salary boost.

The woman with an advanced business degree will find it of greatest use to her within the first five years of graduation. She must take care to utilize its impact to the fullest during that period. As the years pass, the degree becomes an increasingly distant achievement in a what-have-you-done-for-me-lately world.

Whether a woman with a decade of work experience under her belt should leave the work force, earn an M.B.A. and return is a very individual question and one open to great debate. One woman, a success in a major corporation while only in her mid-thirties, confides that she gave heavy consideration to returning to school for a graduate business degree to give a boost to her career. "I decided not to get it and I'm glad now," says the woman, whose salary is about $75,000 a year. "Business is fickle. In the seventies it was all for M.B.A.'s. Today's push is for graduate engineering and technology degrees. I don't think an M.B.A. would make a big difference in my future now." She had decided against working for any advanced degree. Instead, she continually updates her education with night courses in economics and computer technology. A political science major in college, she has already enhanced her career with accounting and public-speaking courses. Instead of second-guessing her educational background anymore, she is committed to making the most of the expertise she already has.

GROWTH VERSUS NO-GROWTH COMPANIES

The successful woman recognizes that some industries are growing by leaps and bounds and others are in decay.

It is only common sense for a woman to position herself in a growing company in a growth industry. When a company experiences rapid growth, there are more management opportunities available. The experienced woman can find new challenges to grow and test herself. Moreover, she has many opportunities for mobility if her competitors are growing rapidly also. She knows that good management is hard to find and that growth industries are hard-pressed to develop management fast enough.

Thus, in the mid-1980s the executive woman keeps her eye on high-technology industries, computer sales and diversification, as well as industries that provide services related to improving corporate productivity. She is not attracted to the steel or the automobile industry. She knows that contracting industries are eliminating management positions rather than creating new ones. She also is well aware that it is a far, far harder deed to persuade management to give her a hefty salary increase—no matter how stellar her performance—if the company is not making a profit.

Growing Industries	Contracting Industries
Advertising	Aerospace
Apparel—Fashion—Retailing	Agriculture
Airlines, regional	Airlines, national
Banking and Financial services	Automobiles and trucks and tires
Broadcasting	Industrial services
Cable TV	Metals and Steel
Chemical engineering	Railroads

Computers and Electronics
Health care and Medical
services
High technology
Personal care
Real estate and Housing
Telecommunications

Unions
Utilities

BUSINESSES THAT ENCOURAGE WOMEN

There are certain industries in which women are more accepted at higher levels. Retailing management, consumer products, publishing, computer design, information processing, advertising and banking have less resistance to promoting women to executive positions. Diversified financial service companies, including banks and insurance, have been receptive to promoting women.

The industrial sector has permitted the fewest women in its upper ranks. While retail industry has promoted women to lower-middle and middle management, it has been reluctant to move them to the top level of management.

"Smokestack America," the heavy industrial sector, has undergone a severe contraction in the past few years, greatly diminishing its appeal for the ambitious upcoming woman. In a way, the tables have turned: For decades industrial America has resisted hiring women, and now savvy women are rejecting it and opting for greener pastures. Since the Western world's economy is becoming more service-oriented, a woman would do well to concentrate on a service business.

ENTRY-LEVEL JOBS

The ideal company to get in with is a company rapidly growing in a growth industry. The woman who is serious about building a successful career looks for jobs that open doors to myriad future opportunities. There is a wide variety of different avenues to enter the corporate world. The successful woman tries to position herself in a job that will serve as a strong jumping-off point for her travels up the corporate ladder:

Management trainee. If a company has a management training program, it can be invaluable. A good program offers the person entering the work force a chance to look at the various aspects of the company and see what appeals to her most. She picks a company with an excellent program. The management program trains her to become a manager of a department section. As she proves herself she takes on larger and larger responsibilities.

Sales trainee/Sales assistant. This is a prized position for the young woman beginning her career. Usually these jobs pay miserably, but she sacrifices because she knows she's orienting her career in the right direction. After she finishes the training, she begins to sell on her own—and has an opportunity to earn commissions.

Executive assistant. This is an advantageous position *if* the executive is willing to delegate and let the young assistant try her wings. If the executive is truly powerful, the young assistant can make invaluable contacts for future career moves. Moreover, this job can lead to an important promotion if the young assistant performs well. She is highly visible to the executive who brought her in and to other senior managers. When a job opens, her skills are already a known factor.

Front desk hotel manager. In the hotel industry, a specialized degree in hotel management is advisable. But this is still a place where the determined, clever woman can find her way to the top. From a highly visible job managing the front desk, she expands to catering services and convention sales. When she becomes assistant hotel manager, she adds responsibility for housekeeping, maintenance, buying and accounting. Becoming hotel manager in a chain of hotels is the beginning of a highly mobile career as an executive managing numbers of hotels.

Quality control inspector. Quality control is a critical function in high-tech companies. A woman can advance from QC inspection to shift manager to director of quality assurance. This leads her over to manufacturing responsibilities and senior production avenues.

Note: Quality control is an area often open to women. Advancement takes not only superior skills, but determination.

Word processor. The woman who has superior data processing skills for operating state-of-the art glorified typewriters has a jump on the woman who has considerably more experience but who is intimidated by the 2001 equipment moving into the offices. The savvy word processor has a background which can serve as basis for promotion in rapidly expanding data processing.

Writer, magazines and newspapers. Writing is a line job at many magazines and publications, which routinely look for promising young managers among their writing staffs.

Executive secretary. This is still a difficult starting position in a company because executives so prize an excellent secretary that they are reluctant to promote her. Being an executive secretary is an excellent way for a young woman to learn business procedures and to study the nature of the company she is working in. She should at the very first interview indicate that she is interested in the job as a learning experience and would after a period of time like to advance to a position of increased responsibility.

Even after she advances, a young woman will find that some of the male staff will still refer to her as "So-and-so's secretary." Her best bet is to take the promotion, get some interesting experience under her belt and move to another organization. There she will enter the company as junior management, untainted by the stigma that sometimes follows ex-secretaries in their old organizations.

OUTSIDE POSITIONS

The company a woman chooses for her first more responsible job might be one that provides services for other corporations. Such firms provide an unobstructed view into the inner workings of a variety of client companies. Moreover, the ambitious woman makes a wide variety of contacts that can assist her future career.

Accounting. Joining a consulting accounting firm as top-notch as possible is one way for a woman to gain visibility with the upper management of several companies. She enhances her prospects of being offered an important position while gaining her a chance to study the management style of a company so that she is likely to pick one where she fits in.

Art. In-house art departments are rarely appreciated. Management tends to value outside work. Working on the outside of a company, an artist is able to charge a much higher fee for a job well done.

Investment banking. Mergers and acquisitions are negotiated at the highest level. The woman specializes in putting together corporate partnerships. If she is good, her visibility with top management is sensational.

Outside legal counsel. This woman specializes in corporate or international law and is brought in to consult on mergers and acquisitions or to prevent unwanted takeover bids. Once again, she tries to deal with the top brass of any company she counsels. She seeks opportunities to win and be proven prudent in front of everyone.

Management consulting. Again, she picks a firm with a prestigious reputation that is typically hired by senior management of large firms. More than once a board of directors has decided to ditch inadequate management and to hire the bright management consultant they had brought in to critique the corporate performance.

Banking. Corporate finance can lead to top management contact at major corporations. Creative finance packages impress management hierarchies.

LINE VERSUS STAFF

Once on the inside of a company, the successful woman is careful to avoid dead-end jobs, something many women in the past forgot to consider. A staff job is a financial liability to the company. It requires corporate money for its offices, salaries, benefits, and expenses without contributing directly into the corporate kitty. It is a cost center.

On the other hand, line experience is work with responsibility for and authority over employees who are producing something that generates revenues for the company. A line job is a profit center.

Frequently, a woman starts out in a staff job (indeed, often it's unavoidable) and then moves to a line. A staff job, if she is reporting to a key executive, can be beneficial for the short haul. For instance, it can give a woman an overall view of the company she works for. "I started staff and then moved over to sales after a couple of years. The staff job developed my confidence," ventures New York banker Adelaide A. Sink. "The staff job was a less visible arena where I spent a couple of years figuring out how to play the game," she continues. "People who go directly into sales may develop arrogance. They may not understand that some staff backup is essential. I now understand the two parts need each other."

Recalls a communications executive: "My biggest single move was going from public relations to sales. At first I thought I could never sell. I could never leave staff and move over. Then I thought, maybe I can. After all I was selling my ideas all the time. When I moved to sales I gained confidence because I contributed to the bottom line. I could point to what I had done. No one could argue with me. The money I pulled in told the tale very eloquently."

VELVET GHETTO JOBS

The ghetto is women and the velvet is a salary that looks impressive at first glance. But once in the ghetto it's hard to work your way out. These jobs are not jobs to build from. They are dead ends.

Accountant. Accountants keep track of money other people in the company produced. Their presence is regarded as a necessary evil. They are regarded as part of the cost of doing business. The creative, talented accountant would do better going into the consulting business outside of the company. Senior management at the company always think outside accountants are smarter than the ones they have in-house—partly because of the hefty fees accounting firms charge. In-house accountants are just glorified bookkeepers.

A woman with an accounting degree would do best to work for a prestigious consulting firm and enter a client corporation in finance rather than accounting. Financial vice presidents can be very powerful corporate presences, heavily involved in setting company philosophy.

Architect. Building projects generally overrun their original budgets and eat into corporate profits. There's no way an architect, no matter how charming, talented and resourceful she may be, can demand salary increases if she works for a company, such as a chemical company, that is not primarily in the architecture business. Moreover, architects are practically never promoted up outside their department within industrial companies. They do far better working for an architectural firm whose sole business is architecture or as an independent consultant.

Benefits Administrator. Employee benefits are paid out of profits. This job, no matter how skillfully administered, is a drain on profits. Cutting back the drain a little bit is not a powerful argument for a raise. It is a no-win department.

Buyer or procurer. Once again, this office spends the corporate money. No matter how good a job the buyer does, she is still spending money—not producing it. She is more likely to make an impression on the manufacturers she buys from than to win recognition in the eyes of her own management. The people she negotiates with are much more likely to appreciate the tough bargains she drives.

Chemist. A high-priced employee with little basis for negotiating raises, unless she discovers something that is credited to her directly and that makes the company enough money to get the attention of senior management. Otherwise, she should first aim to manage her department and then move in to general management.

Contract administrator. Another cost center. The person who negotiated the contract gets all the glory. Contract administrators get all the headaches.

Customer service person. Women frequently end up in this dead-end area. In these jobs they are highly visible to customers. Senior management regards this area as a necessary evil that is part of the cost of doing business.

Logistics planner. Regarded as an ivory-tower type, an intellectual tool. Not likely to be considered for management promotions unless she reports directly to the president.

Personnel specialist. Another unappreciated cost center. This sector is viewed as another necessary evil. No matter how many good people a personnel manager hires, she is unlikely to command the respect she deserves from top management. She has little concrete achievement to negotiate salary increases for herself. (The personnel department includes insurance, etc.)

Public relations, community affairs, and government relations specialists. These are convenient jobs for corporations to give women because they involve dealing with the press and are therefore visible. Not only are such departments powerless dead ends, but they give their members no substantive evidence to earn salary increases. Since these positions are highly visible and removed from the mainstream of the company's business, they are the perfect place to put the company's token female executives.

Researchers. This is regarded as a necessary expenditure for assuring future profits. The credit for the product will no doubt go to the marketing department and the bonuses will go to the sales people. The smart researcher moves over to marketing.

Writer. The only writer in a company who gets any top attention is the one who writes the speeches for the boss. This is a positive and highly lucrative position: The boss hears the applause for his speech; this gives the woman writer basis to ask for a raise. Otherwise, it is a thankless positon with no future. Writing is generally viewed as a commodity as common as the pencils that produce it. Writers should consider advertising agencies, which sometimes generously remunerate their stellar copywriters.

GROWTH POSITIONS

The woman executive never forgets the basic premise of the capitalist system: making money. Business is conducted to make a profit. If she contributes to the profits of a company in a quantifiable way, she is never at a disadvantage when it's time to negotiate a salary increase.

She avoids the thankless corporate departments that generate costs and concentrates instead on profit centers. She knows that the best way to get attention from the top is to make money.

"Look at a company and try to determine what is important to that company," advises Adelaide Sink. "Identify the mainstream of that particular company. Go to work in the mainstream. It's more difficult to get the top management's attention working out on a limb."

The heartbeat of any company is its cash flow, so the executive woman positions herself close to the corporate pulse.

Attorney. Having specialized in corporate law or international trade law, the lawyer avoids dead-end aspects of law such as trademarks and contracts and specializes in marketing expansion, mergers and takeovers. "Show me a lawyer who tells me what I can do," mutters a chairman of a large company. "Most of them spend all their time telling what I cannot do." The lawyer on her way up points the corporation in new and more profitable directions.

Advertising, Media buyer. As the world becomes more media-oriented, the demand for careful placement of advertising on radio and television becomes more critical. The progression from media buyer is to media planning and then to media supervisor. From there a woman moves to become a minor account executive and then vice president and major account executive.

Advertising sales, all media. Whether for a local radio or television station, cable TV, or newspaper or magazine advertising, sales is the organization's lifeblood. In a local television station the progression is: sales trainee, salesperson, head of local sales, head of national sales, sales manager, station manager and finally general manager. Then the successful manager looks to a more important station, to a chain of stations or to a network or cable system.

In the magazine or newspaper business the progression is from local sales to a special sales sector, such as liquor and automobiles, to regional sales manager to national sales manager. The next move is to advertising director and from there to associate publisher to publisher.

Note: There is resistance everywhere against moving women from secretarial or editorial positions into sales. A woman would do best beginning in a sales assistant job.

Computer expert. As the world becomes increasingly electronically wired the computer expert becomes more necessary, particularly in banking and finance, where the money moves around the globe with the flick of a button. The ambitious computer maven chooses a company where the computer is the artificial heart that pumps the corporate blood—and she is indispensable.

The trip upward has many steps:

Typist
Word processor
Computer operator
Computer operations manager
Computer programmer
Computer software designer
Computer analyst
Manager of information systems
Vice president in charge of technical services

When people talk about a future in data processing, they are serious.

Contract negotiator. Whether negotiating unions or sales, the shrewd negotiator gets attention from the very top. If she negotiates a hefty profit margin on a sales contract, she has fodder for her own salary demands. If she manages the delicate balance between union peace and increased corporate profitability, her company will give her, gratefully, whatever it takes to keep her happily employed. She reminds her management from time to time how much a strike would cost. Being the marvelous negotiator she is, she structures hefty wage increases for herself. She is so good at it that the boss is smiling as he or she accepts her terms.

Engineer. Armed with an engineering degree, a woman can advance through management designing new products that will enrich the corporate coffers.

Geologist. This position can impact the bottom line directly if a company is in the natural resource business. A good geologist can save an oil company hundreds of millions of dollars in wasted drilling and digging costs. When it is time for salary review, the geologist exhibits figures showing how much money the company garnered from developing the sites she suggested.

Further, she compares her track record to the industry average, demonstrating that her skill accounts for the difference.

Loan officer. This position is highly visible to senior management if a woman is able to create high-yielding loans in competitive, aggressive markets. She charms her clients with her superior "people skills" and manages to obtain favorable exposure from her own bank's senior management as well as with the client companies' management. This can lead to a bank vice presidency and loan responsibility for a geographical region. She aims at overall national loan management and a senior vice presidency. By then, who knows? Maybe the world will be ready for a female bank president of a bank that was founded by men.

Medical managers. There are top-level management jobs available to trained medical doctors and registered nurses. These jobs require that their education be used not in direct medical practice but in management as a health care administrator. Medical care systems are a growth area for the foreseeable future. The nurse or doctor with management skills or the M.B.A. with some medical background will have many new executive opportunities.

New product developer. This position is valuable only if the woman in charge has selected and correctly positioned new products in the marketplace. If she has cornered a significant market share and her product brings money to the bottom line, she needs only call attention to the dollars-and-cents figures to write her own bonus check.

Restaurant manager. As a manager of a franchise restaurant in a growing chain of restaurants, a woman has a chance to build a profit center that is unequivocally hers. Success at one outlet leads to opportunities to manage two or three outlets in the area. There she may be invited to manage increasingly large geographic sectors. This could lead to an executive marketing position in the chain's senior management.

This career has two advantages. First, restaurant chains frequently have their own in-house management training programs to maximize the abilities of their managers. Second, this is a highly competitive industry with high visibility for any achiever. Super-performers are courted from one company to the next. The successful woman will receive regular solicitations from other firms that will give her an extra weapon when it is time to negotiate compensation.

Retail promotion specialists. In the past, buying has been a traditional path to merchandise store management. Now promotion is receiving increasing credit for retail sales success. Good buying no longer has all the recognition for sales. The promotion campaign gets much of the credit at the pace-setting retail stores.

The successful promoter is highly visible in any store where she operates and in the chain of stores. Moreover, as in any intensely competitive industry, the successful woman is paid heed to by her competitors.

Salespersons and marketers. These positions have been the crux of American business for the past half century. Whether the product is insurance, stocks and bonds, management services, computers, fast food, airplanes, television spots, oil or razor blades, sales is the heart of a business.

A saleswoman has concrete evidence of how valuable she has been to the company she works for. A sales manager has a team whose performance she takes credit for. To prove her worth and get the attention of the president of the company, all she has to do is add up how much she brought to the company till.

Frequently, the top salesperson in an organization is the highest-paid person there. Since money and success assure respect from men, the successful sales and marketing executive has it made.

It's when she wants to move up that the successful salesperson may find resistance. While her male sales peer has a good chance of moving up through sales management into general line management, the woman may find resistance. She has to be alert to the mood of her company and judge whether senior management is psychologically ready to promote a woman to manage a predominantly male sales staff.

2 LANDING THE POSITION

Regardless of which area of business a woman chooses for her career, she has to aggressively seek out the job she wants. Great jobs are not likely to fall into her lap. She has to find them and work toward them. She also has to let the companies know she exists. If they have never heard about her they are not going to look her up in the phone directory and call her.

Often the first impression a woman makes on a prospective employer is a piece of paper with her life history sketchily described for management to see. Whether it gets tossed in the wastepaper basket (or placed into a "file" which is about the same thing) or gets her in the front door is something over which a woman has control. It is critical for her to know this so she will present herself effectively.

COVER LETTER

More important than the resume in getting the employer's initial attention is the cover letter, says the chairman of the board of a big and rapidly growing New York–based company. "Anybody can say 'Enclosed is my resume and I will be calling you for an interview.' Well, that's not saying enough. The cover letter is the key attention-getter. It has to be direct, short and creative." The busy executive adds that he is impressed with a persistent applicant who asks for any five minutes at any time.

FOLLOW-UP

The follow-up to the letter and the resume is crucial. The applicant should not wait to hear from the company, but should initiate a telephone call to the person she sent the resume to. She should keep calling until she gets a definite no for an answer. "The worst thing she can do is say, I'll wait to hear from you," notes a high-powered executive who has little time to think about calling job applicants.

Most executives respect tenacity. "If a woman goes after a job with flair and persistence, she's likely to go after a big contract the same way. I like that," says a top male executive.

After she has sent a successful cover letter and persistently called to see that her letter and resume were sent to the right person's attention, the resume itself comes under scrutiny.

THE RESUME

FOCUS

A woman who is uncertain of which way she wants her career to turn may write her resume several different ways, each focusing on certain connected aspects of her work history. For instance, a managing editor of a business periodical who wants to move into business would stress the management aspects of her job, how many people reported to her, what systems she initiated, the growth of the publication during her tenure and her broad exposure to the business community.

On the other hand, if she wishes to continue in the publishing business, she stresses the deadline record of her staff and her relationship with the printing and distribution backup.

The focus must be consistent through the description of each job. Successful women make it easy for employers to see the logic of their career patterns.

RESUME CHRONOLOGY

The applicant lists her most recent job and her most recent title first on her resume. She describes succinctly the responsibilities that relate directly to the job she is applying for. She states her pertinent accomplishments unabashedly. No one else is going to be standing next to her prospective employer when the letter and resume arrive to assure that B. J., the boss, knows she is terrific. B. J. has to sense competence in the pithy descriptions of what the applicant has done. The most recent job generally is the one described in most detail. The second most recent job follows, with the dates she held it, her boss's title and the company and location.

As an applicant regresses back over her career, the descriptions become so brief they may disappear—job titles may be an adequate description.

LENGTH

The resume should not be over one page if the applicant is under thirty-five. Often a well-written application for a woman of any age can be condensed to one page. If the woman has importantly distinguished herself, two pages may be necessary to describe her career. Under no circumstances, even if she has been a Cabinet Secretary, does a woman routinely submit more than two pages for her resume.

OTHER RESUME INFORMATION

- Educational institutions: Fields of study and additional independent studies are pertinent.
- Organizations and honors: The successful woman does not hide her candle under a basket. If she was voted most outstanding in her community, she puts that information down on her resume. Elected offices she has held in professional organizations give her an air of industry prominence.
- Hobbies: These are listed only if they reveal something about the personality of the applicant. If she sailed the Atlantic solo in an eighteen-foot boat, it indicates she is disciplined and self-sufficient. If she wins marathons, it indicates she is disciplined and fit. No one cares about her needlepoint unless she is an expert looking for employment at a textile company.
- Age: Many women omit any reference to their age on their resume. While they list the dates of previous employment, they omit the dates of graduation from college and high school and their date of birth. "I'm forty-five but everyone thinks I'm closer to thirty-five," declares one executive woman who recently went through the job-hunting process without revealing her age. "After they see me, the first impression of vitality remains even after they find out my true age."

RESUME BUZZ WORDS

Even if a woman knows precious little about business, certain buzz words on her resume imply a familiarity with business priorities.

- "Responsibility" or "Responsibilities included" or "Full responsibility" or "Overall responsibility" or "Line responsibility" or "Complete responsibility"
- "Profit" or "Profitability" or "Profit growth" or "Profit center" or "Enhanced profitability"
- "Designed and implemented" or "Initiated and executed" or "Executed successfully"
- "Budgetary responsibilities"
- "Cost containment" or "Cost reduction" or "Simplified with considerable cost reductions"
- "On-target performance" or "Ahead of schedule"
- "Information system"
- "In-house"
- "Updated" or "Streamlined" or "Modernized" or "Introduced efficiency"
- "Successfully executed" or "Successfully implemented"

JOB INTERVIEWS

How a woman conducts herself during an interview can make a major difference as to whether she is the successful candidate for the job she wants in today's tough job market.

DRESSING FOR JOB INTERVIEWS

First impressions can have lasting effects, and how a woman presents herself for a job interview is critical. Since she wants to be taken seriously, she dresses seriously, selecting her clothes with great care.

HOW A SUCCESSFUL APPLICANT PRESENTS HERSELF:

- She does wear a sedate dress or suit—it looks more serious.
- She does dress conservatively—the successful woman wants to have her face remembered, not her dress.
- She does wear minimal jewelry—too much jewelry can make her look too affluent. A strand of pearls and a few pieces of gold jewelry are adequate.
- She does pay attention to her fingernails—her hands are between her and the interviewer. She does not want her hands to detract from her image.
- She does wear neat, shiny, clean hair back off of her face—faces are more serious than hair.
- She does wear clear red lipstick.
- She does coordinate shoes and accessories carefully—she doesn't want to be remembered for her green shoes.
- She does organize the briefcase tidily—whipping out a resume or other papers on cue subtly conveys efficiency and power.
- She does take medication if she has a cold—sniffles are not powerful.
- She does arrive at least one minute early.

THINGS A SUCCESSFUL APPLICANT DOESN'T DO

- She doesn't put lunch in her briefcase.
- She doesn't carry a big purse.
- She doesn't wear nail polish or lipstick that calls attention to itself.
- She doesn't wear bright eye shadow—office lights can distort a color that looks lovely in other lighting to a harsh or glaring tone.
- She doesn't wear cheap jewelry.
- She doesn't wear anything filmy or slinky.
- She doesn't wear a red dress.
- She doesn't dig in her purse to find a pencil.
- She doesn't wear a hat—the interviewer will wonder if there is a reason, e.g., baldness.

- She doesn't wear bows or ribbons in her hair.
- She doesn't take her jacket off during the interview—jackets are powerful.
- She doesn't ask for a piece of paper to write on. She whips out a carefully organized pad.
- She doesn't smoke—the interviewer may be offended by smoking. The need to smoke during an interview makes the applicant appear less disciplined.
- She doesn't wear heavy perfume.
- She doesn't eat garlic or onions before the interview.
- She doesn't chew gum.
- She doesn't complain about the chill if it's too cool.
- She doesn't show off her figure.
- She doesn't wear pants.

MANAGING THE INTERVIEW

The successful woman never walks into a corporate personnel office for an interview before she has researched the nature of the company. She knows its strengths and weaknesses in its industry.

First of all, she must remember that the interview is an opportunity to talk. It is her first chance to reveal herself, the person behind the resume and the phone calls. She does not need to discuss the facts on her resume— those have already been digested by her possible employer. The successful woman uses the interview to demonstrate that she is the kind of fine potential employee the company wants to hire.

INTERVIEW WITH PERSONNEL

The savvy woman distinguishes between her interview with the personnel department and the one with her prospective boss. There are subtle differences. While she is courteous and thorough with the personnel department, the successful woman is aware that her prospective boss is the one who has the last say when it comes to hiring her. How well she relates to the person she will report to often may be far more important than how popular she is in the personnel department. At upper management levels, the interview by the personnel department may be only token since her prospective boss may have already solicited her for the job.

Moreover, as a woman becomes an executive herself she may find that her salary requirements far exceed those of the personnel people interviewing her. This sometimes makes the interview less pleasant, since personnel employees, being human, are susceptible to jealousy. The successful woman is on guard for a slightly hostile interview and tries to help her interviewer become less defensive.

Regardless of who is interviewing her, however, the interview is an excellent opportunity for a woman to position herself carefully for the desired job and to put herself in the best possible light. It is essential that she communicate that she is a self-starter with much to offer.

It is critical that she does not clam up. "The worst thing anyone can do in an interview is to come in, sit down, and then not talk," observes Dolores White, a broadcast industry executive whose responsibilities include being in charge of personnel. She stresses the importance of an applicant's opening up so that she can get a feel for the kind of employee the applicant would be. "I'm the silent end of the interview," notes Ms. White. "I want them to talk."

INTERVIEW WITH THE BOSS

Women would do well to practice their interview as a semimonologue with friends until they have developed positive, interesting ten-minute responses to the following four basic questions. (Chances are they will need only five minutes of the information for the interview, but they should have more up their sleeve in case they have a chance to use it.) If they are not asked for this information, they volunteer it.

1. "Tell me about yourself." (This is an opportunity for a woman to reveal much about what kind of a person she is.)

She may elect to mention:
- Sports participation and athletic activities
- Hobbies and crafts she enjoys
- Musical instruments she plays
- Concerts she attended recently
- Interest in drama or the arts
- Vacation places and activities
- Pets
- Gardening
- Favorite books recently read
- Clubs and organizations she is active in
- Civic activities she is involved with

She should not mention:
- Her sick grandmother
- The burglary at her house
- Flat tire on the way to the interview
- Her husband and three children, except in passing
- Recent attempt to lose weight
- Hassles of juggling career with home life
- Any recent illness or accident
- The worst thing about her last job

- Her allergies
- Religion
- The fact that she is a tectotaler
- The fact that she is a vegetarian

2. "What can you contribute to this particular company?" Once again, the applicant should steer away from what is on her resume and speak more generally. This gives her an opportunity to discuss:
- Her personal enthusiasm for work.
- Important industry contacts—people who like her. She does not drop the names of her enemies.
- Important community connections.
- Her knowledge of the industry—perceived strengths and weaknesses.
- How she can contribute to the company's overall success, making it even stronger in specific areas. "Contribute" is a key buzz word for interviews. "Workers are a dime a dozen," notes personnel executive White, "but contributors are what I'm looking for. They are not easy to find."

3. "What can you contribute to the position that is available. Why do you want to work for this company?" This is where the woman gets more specific about her own skills and talents and her research on the company. She mentions:
- Previous achievements she can surpass or duplicate
- Familiarity with the nature of the work
- How she can strengthen the position
- Perceived pitfalls in the position and how to avoid them
- How her previous experience ties in with the position
- Why she is perfect for the job

4. "Why do you want to leave your present job for a new one here?" Once again, the woman does not have to mention that she hates her boss, finds the job undoable or cannot get along with a co-worker. She does not discuss the political wars. She focuses on the positive. She does not mention that money is a major factor in her departure. Future employers are looking for employees who espouse loyalty, not the ones who will hop to the next employer for another $10 a week. She discusses:
- Her need for greater challenges
- Her desire to learn and grow
- Her appreciation of the company interviewing her
- How her skills can be put to better use
- Her reluctance to leave the other employer balanced against her need to seek new opportunities

STRAIGHT OUT OF SCHOOL

Kae Peet, an executive who screens thousands of young people's resumes looking for likely candidates for a much-coveted training program she runs in the television business, says the resume can be crucial to a candidate's success. She immediately dismisses resumes or letters with typos or poor grammar. "If the person says, 'I hope to hear from you,' they won't," comments Peet. "I don't have time to call them. They have to call me."

Joining the work force can be humbling, notes Peet. "A student may have done wonderfully in school but when she is out in the job market she has to start as the low person on the totem pole."

Observes New York television executive Dolores White, "If they call me up and tell me, 'I don't have any business experience and I want a job,' I'm already impressed. The fact that they have enough guts and initiative to call me up cold shows me that they are not afraid of the business world."

TIPS FOR WRITING THE FIRST RESUMÉ

- Arrange the information nicely on the page.
- Write concisely about ambitions and experience.
- List all work experience, concentrating on jobs that required initiative and entailed some pressure.
- Itemize Christmas holiday and part-time jobs.
- List extracurricular activites.
- Indicate career objectives.
- List important school honors.
- Write three different resumes each with a different business focus. (This is particularly important for young people who have not decided which areas of business are most interesting to them.)
- Begin the job search during the final year of school. Beat the June rush.

PART TWO

ROUTE
TO THE
TOP

Executive women are not Pollyannas about succeeding in essentially still-male bastions. They know the deck is stacked against them. They know they have to work extra hard to compensate for the residual doubt in the male business community about the extent of women's commitment to their career. These women know that the older generation of men is probably full of silent resentment over women leaving home and working outside of the pink collar world. Sixty-year-old men were born in 1923 to parents who were born in the nineteenth century. Their Victorian attitudes come as no surprise.

Instead of being angry and resentful about the extra hurdles between them and success, smart women take action. They make every effort to cultivate the men who dislike them the most. They woo their most adamant detractors. They overcompensate by being absolutely above reproach in their office and working lives. Importantly, they take a long-term view of the opposition to their upward progress. In five years the sixty-year-olds will be retiring. In twenty years the forty-year-olds will be sixty. Forty-year-old men have a much more positive mind set about the role of women in business. Successful women keep their perspective.

3 BEATING HER LEGACY

It was not by accident that the executive woman became an executive. She made it to the top because she's excellent at what she does. She regards her job the way an athlete regards her training. "When you get that chance to run the all-important race, you'd better be ready to win," declares an industrial executive. "You train and train and when the big break comes you go for it."

"I like doing everything I do. I'd do this job even if I had a million dollars to spare," is the enthusiastic assessment of executive life by Elaine Linker, vice president of a New York–based television firm. Her enthusiasm is typical of the woman who makes it to the top. One of the reasons successful women become successful is that they have found their niche and it feels comfortable. The long hours and tough responsibilities they carry on their silk-shirted shoulders are actually pleasurable for them.

"My whole life is my business. It's not like work to me. It's not work—it's fun and I love it," echoes Doris Mattus-Hurley, president of Haagen-Dazs Franchise, Inc. in New Jersey. These two women are married, have children, toil twelve to fifteen hours a day and love it.

"The best way to make it to the top is to do something you absolutely enjoy. If you don't enjoy it or like it you never will make it up there," notes Sandra Meyer, president of the Communications Division of American Express. The business world, however, is still very much a man's world. "If a man and a woman with equal background and qualifications were in competition for the same job the man would likely get it," states a top-ranked woman. "That's why a woman has to be more equal. She has to be better. That's all there is to it."

STARTING WITH THE DISADVANTAGES

Being a woman in business is a large disadvantage for the ambitious manager. To offset it she has to be very, very good. The easiest way to be good—better than her competing male counterparts—is to enjoy her work.

In business, women do not have the luxury of scoring anything but straight 10's on a scale from 1 to 10. At the outset simply by being a woman they enter the arena with one miserable 3 already entered on their score card. Either they score straight 10's on everything else or they're out of the running.

THE NOVICE POLITICIAN

The woman entering the management arena has a major disadvantage that the males at her company don't have. She is a novice at politics and power plays. "I'm an ambitious person but I was not a business school person," notes an executive at a prestigious Wall Street investment firm. "Because I didn't go to business school I didn't have a network when I arrived here. Most of the men, on the other hand, had better backgrounds for business, went to B. school, knew what they wanted and knew each other."

"Knowing" each other means they have had an opportunity to size each other up—not as friends but as possible allies and competitors in the corporate arena. "Knowing" means they have evaluated the strengths and weaknesses of the other guys, developed a strategy for emerging as the leader of the pack, and decreased the chances of any political sabotage.

"The corporation is a tribal society," observes Dr. Dorothy Gregg, a trailblazing executive who for several years was vice president of Celanese, a three-billion-dollar-a-year industrial company. "Unless the woman understands the socialization factor and is gradually introduced to society, ostracism will result. A young man entering the company will be instructed for two years on 'how it is done around here.' The young woman probably won't." A young man will be made subtly aware of who is a comer and who is on the way out. He'll be instructed as to who goofed last year and who scored a coup. "Go to lunch with J. R.," he'll be told. He knows that means J. R. is a possible ally. The young man will be told many tiny things that add up to a lot of information—and an extra rung or two on the ladder of success.

One woman compares her sense of exclusion from the male network to being in a baseball game where all the other players know the signals and she does not. "I'm up at bat and the pitcher is signaling what kind of ball he's going to pitch and the catcher is signaling back and I don't know what the signals mean. If I could read them I'd know what kind of ball I was going to be thrown and I could prepare to deal with it before the pitch was made. But I don't know the signals. So when the ball is thrown my reactions have got to be extra fast since I have no idea what I'm about to receive."

"Politics" in a corporate sense is essentially the perception of relationships between various aspects of management and subtle differences in pecking order. It means knowing where the bodies are buried and observing who is a designated standard bearer and who is on the way out.

Politics means hearing not only what is said but also what is meant.

Politics is listening to what is *not* said as closely as to what is said. It entails analyzing who in fact has how much power and who is likely to have it in the future. Politics is subtle craftiness. The bottom line is power. The woman who combines political savvy with her superior smarts gets to grab the golden ring.

The political woman does not look for friends in the corporation. The rules are different in the corporate arena. She looks for allies. Political women understand that doing business with people is not the same as dealing with them in the outside world, where loyalties are forged and friends and enemies are placed in separate camps. Like Washington politics, corporate politics sometimes makes for strange bedfellows.

"At first I didn't want to admit to being a political creature," confides a senior woman in the communications industry. "That was dumb of me. You can be very political and there is nothing wrong with it. You just don't talk about it." She has put her finger on an essential aspect of corporate politics: The wise corporate woman never admits to being a political beast. She is not a gossip or a rumor bearer.

Corporate politics is a game never verbally acknowledged. If you emerge on the top rungs of the corporate ladder everyone knows you played your politics well—but no one ever calls it by name.

THE CLOSET HOMEMAKER

One of the strikes automatically called against a woman entering management ranks is a legacy left her by previous female managers who have opted out of the office for the home. Whenever this occurs, a distrust for a woman's seriousness about her career automatically transfers to other women in the company.

One instance of a star woman trading her career for home life, and a thousand subsequent striving women have to work twice as hard to convince their bosses that they are serious.

Women themselves have not completely shaken the stereotypical notion that they are imbued with in our current culture: that after they finish college they will work a few years and then leave the office arena to get married. Even today, many women themselves do not accept that most of them are going to work in offices all of their lives.

"Women tend to think in terms of there being a way out for them. They tend to think they can always find a man to marry and then quit," notes a president who worked initially to support her children.

Even the daughter of a hard-driving executive mother does not escape this age-old concept, observes her mother candidly. "My son knows he has no choice," she says. "He doesn't think he can always get married and have children and opt out. But my daughter (twenty-four years old and working as a commodities trader) has way back in her head a residual feeling that 'I can always get married and quit. There's a way out.' She thinks in terms of a possible alternative."

As long as executive women continue to discard their careers to marry and keep house for Mr. Right, all other women will be forced to go that extra mile to prove their commitment to their career.

THE TEMPTRESS

Not only does the male-dominated corporate world seize on isolated instances of women abandoning their careers as an excuse to doubt the dedication of the millions of women who stick to their jobs until retirement; it absolutely fixates on the woman who goes to bed with her boss.

"One instance of a junior executive sleeping with a senior guy who is estranged from his wife, and the men I work with are looking at me and saying, 'Who did you sleep with to get this job?' " laments a woman who inched her way up the corporate ladder with twenty years of twelve-hour workdays. Every time a star reporter moves in with the publisher or a president denies he is having an affair with a woman vice president who reports to him, women throughout the world are subjected to new scrutiny and sexual innuendo. One woman goes to bed with one man and makes national headlines. The fallout sets up millions of working women for comments denigrating not only their good taste but their effectiveness on the job.

"It seems that men just don't want to believe that women can get out there, plug away at a job for years and get ahead just like men do," sighs one woman. "If you're beautiful and talented it's harder to prove you're serious," laments a beautiful and talented vice president.

Because of her undeniably professional executive appearance and decorum, the successful woman is clearly not a "party girl." She obviously is "all business." She is never coy and she is deliberately nonseductive. Moreover, she avoids situations that could be construed as in any way compromising. Anticipating and deliberately avoiding romantic overtones is her best defense.

If, in spite of all a woman's efforts to keep a man's attention focused on business, an insensitive colleague suggests a sexual liaison, the executive woman who is married has the easiest excuse—her husband. "Are you crazy?" she smiles. "You know I adore my Larry." The subject of sex is dismissed as unthinkable.

If the woman has no husband or fiancé or involvement she invents one if at all possible. "I'm very much in love with someone," she lies convincingly.

If the woman is a solo act and the sexually minded man knows she is unattached, she takes the old-fashioned out: "I'm terribly old-fashioned about sex and marriage." Chances are marriage is the farthest thing from her colleague's mind. She is absolutely firm and believable. He has no option but to relent.

If her colleague then wants to marry her, she smiles sadly and sweetly and says, "My work is too important to me. I know I don't have time in my life for a husband right now. It just wouldn't be fair to you. But I'm unbelievably flattered."

Under any circumstances, the solicited woman dismisses the sexual overture as quickly and as lightly as possible. She refuses to acknowledge any references to it her colleague may make in the future. She takes special care to avoid circumstances under which the issue can be easily raised again. Further, she takes care to conceal any anger she feels and to keep her business relationship with the man as free from hostility as she possibly can.

The ambitious competent woman in today's office is at a disadvantage: Many men often just don't know how to relate to her. She is constantly in the position of teaching them how. She takes an unflagging sense of humor and persistent gentleness to the office as she slowly educates her colleagues that she is a woman, not a "girl."

Today's executive woman is stuck with the task of being an educator. She is most efficient at educating the men she comes into contact with if she deals pleasantly and patiently with the interchange. Otherwise she risks being simply pigeonholed as a "bitch who insists on wearing the pants in the office."

When her colleague says, "How come you're so cute?" she smiles and says, "Thanks, I wish you'd notice how smart I am too." When the line is, "You're so gorgeous, how come you're not married?" she says, "Thanks, I just can't find a man who will marry me and be my wife," or, "That's interesting. How come I never thought of it?" and changes the subject. If she is called "young lady" she smiles and says, "Thanks. I wish I felt young."

Her patience and good humor combined with her excellent business acumen will make it far easier for the next successful woman her colleagues interact with.

RISK TAKING

It's important to have a chance to do something new, to grow. Thirty-three-year old Judith Moncrieff, manager of Research and Production at Mobil, credits her current success to a job she landed early in her career. "I reported directly to the head of the firm. I ended up doing things that were well beyond my experience. I had a broad exposure to the business community and was always stretching to try to measure up to assignments my boss gave. It was absolutely miserable for me at the time. I was always having to give one hundred percent in order to be able to measure up. I learned to do things I never imagined I could do," Ms. Moncrieff recalls. "Most importantly I learned not to panic regardless of what goes wrong. And I learned how to find out how to do things that seemed initially undoable."

The most successful women have discovered that not only do they need to have the opportunity to fail; they need the growing room to try new tasks and discover their strengths.

Don't be afraid to challenge yourself. "Early on I asked my department head to let me test myself. I said, 'Rather than taking the safe course, let me find out what I can do. I won't let it get you in trouble. I promise to let you know when I need help. Just let me try new things,' " recalls Mary Jane Raphael, an ABC vice president. She was granted her wish, and that was the beginning of her ascent to the top. "You'll never be successful if you don't have some idea of what your abilities are. Everyone is quick to tell you your limitations. Don't be foolhardy but do stretch out," she advises.

Allow for options not previously considered. "If you are too specific about what you think you want to do, sometimes you opt yourself out of something you don't know about," observes a banker whose passage to the executive corridors was triggered by a sudden vacancy in an area she had never considered prior to being offered the job. She resisted her urge to turn it down. She took it and excelled at tasks she had never before thought about handling. The momentum of her success in that unexpected post propelled her to the top.

"I like action," avers E. Camron Cooper, Atlantic Richfield's treasurer. She says action keeps her from being bored.

When in familiar territory, look for the unexplored path. Sometimes getting ahead entails creative learning in areas a woman has never previously considered. "I can find something positive in any job. There's always something you can learn. Sometimes going after offbeat topics and expertises gives you an advantage," comments Colombe Nicholas.

Be open to relocation. Many women are reluctant to step out and take calculated risks. "Women are still so grateful when they have a good job that they are not willing to take the same risks as men. For instance, they are afraid to relocate," notes an executive who recently relocated. "Once I was willing to pack my bags and move anyplace, anytime, there were all kinds of new opportunities available." Part of the contract she negotiated was that her home condominium would be maintained for her in Chicago while she moved to the company's Houston headquarters. "I can visit my friends in Chicago on weekends occasionally," she says.

Another executive says she panicked when she was offered the move from a smaller city to New York City. She was afraid she wasn't good enough to make it there. Her president urged her to accept, saying, "You're getting a chance to play in the big time. Until now you've been in the minor leagues." She decided to move and is enjoying greater success than she imagined. That move, she believes, was the critical factor in her career. In retrospect she wonders why she ever hesitated.

A recent study by a major employer indicates that women do not get very many opportunities to relocate. It reveals that only three out of ten female executives have been asked to relocate, compared with eight out of ten male executives.

There is an important reason why so many more men are offered the opportunity to relocate: Men are moved around when they are being groomed for the top spot in a corporation. When a bright young executive is picked as a potential candidate for the president's office, he is moved so he can experience a wide range of different corporate operations and get an overall view of the company. Then when he is named president he will be familiar with the entire company.

Women are not often being picked as serious candidates for the very top job in American corporations, so corporations don't ask them to make the moves. Why bother to expose them to aspects they are never going to control?

If she wants the control, the executive woman has to be willing to "move!"

Recognize when you've gone as far as you will be allowed to in a particular company. Then move.

"Instead of banging my head against the wall, I look around and find another company willing to take a woman at a higher level," notes a matter-of-fact manager. To gain access to a more powerful position, a woman may make a lateral move over to another company. Occasionally a woman may even take a job at another company that observers may interpret as a step backward. "You don't have to explain what you are doing with your career to everybody," notes senior vice president with Chase Manhattan Elaine Bond. "You'll be vindicated when you make that giant step forward you planned on."

Of course, no move should be made without a lengthy analysis of its long-term implications.

When an ambitious woman encounters the typical prejudice against women in the older male bastion of upper management and perceives resistance against her upward progress, she doesn't make waves. She goes to a headhunter and continues with her old job until she finds a company where her future is brighter. She departs with allies and good feelings in the companies she leaves behind, always careful not to slam doors. In ten years, who knows?

Since there are no barricades barring men from a shot at the president's office, they often spend their entire career at one company. The ambitious woman rarely has that comfortable option. Rather she is forced to move two, three or even four times. Each transfer is to a new company where there is a chance to advance to a position of greater authority and responsibility. She knows most companies have a certain management level above which she will encounter a wall of unspoken but very real resistance.

The ambitious woman is not likely to get discouraged. She looks for a growth job in a growth company in a growing industry. She develops excellent skills. She becomes superb. She learns to be political, she learns the lingo, she learns not to reveal too much about herself. She juggles her family life quietly in the background and participates publicly in civic affairs. She keeps herself trim and healthy. She looks and acts the way the male corporate community expects the perfect corporate woman to look and act. She assesses the mood of her management about promoting her and acts accordingly.

The higher the level at which a woman enters a new company, the more difficult it is for her to win over her male counterparts. Blatant jealousy and sexism constantly dog her. Whenever she joins a firm, she has to prove all over again that she is indeed highly competent and no mere sexist token. The higher she is ranked, the more she is envied.

The successful woman does not delude herself. She is tenacious, political and excellent. Time and again she earns first kudos and ultimately respect. She finds the challenges stimulating. For her, success is both satisfying and addicting. The more power she gains the more she understands why men have been so interested in it. She agrees with what wife, mother and executive Elaine Linker says at the beginning of this section: "I like everything I do. I'd do this job even if I had a million dollars to spare."

RAISES, PERKS AND TITLES

"Women have been so grateful to have their jobs they are afraid to ask for anything more," comments a financial manager. She is probably correct. Women often are timid about pushing for raises or perks. Often, even the more aggressive women wait until their annual review to plead their case for a salary increase.

THE RAISE

The fact is, part of the corporate game has to do with pressing for an increase whenever an executive scores a corporate coup. When an important account is landed, the woman who brought it in should artfully demand an immediate increase—after all, she is immediately more important to the firm. When a critical labor negotiation is settled at terms better than hoped for without a whimper from the union leaders, the woman who negotiated it immediately reminds her superiors of how much money she saved the company and asks for an immediate raise. The savvy corporate woman is not intimidated if her boss says "I didn't budget an increase for you at this point." She points out, "The company didn't budget the windfall I just brought in. Why don't you check it out?" The worst thing that is likely to happen is that the answer will be negative.

Even if she indeed does not get the desired results immediately, the successful woman has brought her excellence to her management's attention. She has made it clear that when her annual review rolls around, the increase should be substantial enough to compensate for her increased value to her company. Companies want to keep their excellent employees happy. The excellent woman has to let her bosses know she knows she is valuable—if not to her company, then to its competitors.

The successful woman knows that part of the game is negotiation: She always asks for more than she expects to get—who knows? She might luck out and get what she asks for! On the other hand, she keeps her requests within the realm of reason.

Negotiating for a Raise

Things She Says	Things She Never Says
• "I contribute to the company's effectiveness."	• "I need the money to pay my bills."
• "These are the things I have done."	• "I've got a family."
	• "I need the money."
• "This is how my performance has improved."	• "You owe it to me."
	• "Other people are making more than I am."
	• "I deserve it because I am still here."
	• "It's only fair that you give it to me."

If she feels that the level of her salary is fair, she expects 2 to 5 percent over the rate of inflation. If inflation is at an annual rate of 7 percent, she asks for a 9 to 12 percent increase. If she receives only a 7 percent raise, she should ask questions about how favorably her performance is viewed. If she receives no increase, she is experiencing a reduction in income in real dollars. This is an important indicator that her services are not appreciated. If her income does not keep up with inflation, she should definitely begin a quiet search for another job where she can make a contribution that will be appreciated.

Importantly, the successful woman pushes for raises with her political radar turned on. She is careful not to bluff too often or overplay her hand. But she is certainly not shy about bringing her success to her management's attention.

PERKS

The ambitious woman knows that many perks are not given out unless they are asked for. She asks.

She routinely negotiates perks along with her salary package. Whether it is first-class plane travel, a limousine to and from the airport, a luxury car rental bracket, a car supplied by the company for her personal use, a rented limousine in another city, unitemized phone calls, discretion in choice of lunch partners and restaurants, or club memberships, she asks. She also asks for credit cards, whether they are for telephone, air travel, car rental or general charge. Perhaps her home phone bill and office paraphernalia are part of her deal.

Negotiating for Perks

Things She Says	Things She Never Says
• "It will facilitate my work."	• "A person in my position deserves it."
• "It saves time."	
• "It saves me."	• "Other people have it."
• "It will permit me to bring prestige to the company and highlight its effectiveness."	• "You do it so I deserve it too."
	• "It is humiliating for me."
• "It is common in our industry and a necessary practice."	
• "My clients expect it."	
• "It facilitates the fact that I work fifteen hour days."	
• "It facilitates my working six days a week."	
• "It cuts down on my paperwork and makes me more efficient."	
• "The company looks bad if I don't do it."	

The successful woman waits for the right time and the right political climate, but she knows that the meek woman inherits the earth. The gutsy woman inherits all the perks.

TITLES

Titles are important. Earning a good salary is a critical factor in being perceived as successful but, further, the executive learned long ago that men respond positively to important titles. A title is particularly effective when she is conducting business in an office other than her own—in her own office, her importance is obvious. "You've got to have that title," says a vice president who is the sole woman officer at her company. "When you are telling some guy he's running his department wrong, the title is absolutely necessary."

If a company won't come up with a hefty raise, the executive negotiates for an improved title in lieu of the raise. She figures she can always take her new title and negotiate a salary increase at a competing company.

4 APPEARING
EXECUTIVE

What distinguishes the very successful executive woman from her secretary or her peers ranked below her in middle management? The super-successful woman has a special executive appearance. She looks successful.

A woman signals who she is by what she wears. "Clothes make a difference in how you feel about yourself and the image you project," declares a broadcast executive.

Men often make snap judgments about a woman's rank and potential by looking at how she presents herself. The woman who wants to be viewed as executive material makes it easy for men to view her in the executive suite.

"Clothes are more important for women than for men. Like it or not, we have to think about what we wear more than men do," states Colombe Nicholas.

For a woman, looking successful means projecting refined understatement in her appearance. In part, this means avoiding calling attention to the fact that she is a woman. Since she is often the only woman present in the boardroom, male peers are already acutely aware of her gender. In order to enhance and strengthen her corporate presence, she is more likely to pad her shoulders than her bra. Shoulders are powerful and the name of the game in the executive suite is power.

Today's in-vogue padded shoulders do more than increase the size of a woman's presence when she is seated at a desk or table (most business is conducted sitting down). They also detract from the size of her bust. The executive woman doesn't want to attract attention to her sexual characteristics any more than her executive male counterpart. She does not need to worry about looking sexy. The successful woman is discovering what men have long known: Success in itself is very sexy. Power is sexy.

The executive concerns herself with looking well-groomed, neat, conservative—and expensive.

There is no reason for the executive woman to underscore her femininity. Being a woman is the worst thing she has going against her in the inner sanctum of the executive suite. The easier she makes it for men to focus on her work, her mind, her ideas and her competence—rather than her gender—the more effective she is as an executive.

Moreover, the executive woman has often found it useful to emulate some of the habits men's life-style and dress have provided them. She does this in a feminine, individual way. She understands that men are threatened when women copy them too closely.

She has lots of pockets, for instance. Men have used pockets for centuries to carry pens, business cards, money and sundry other items, whereas women have carried purses notorious for their clutter.

The executive woman knows that pockets are more efficient than purses. She buys suits and coats with serviceable pockets in which she carries money for tolls, taxis and public transportation. She also tucks in a pen, a small copy of her date book (for making business appointments) and her business cards. For lunch, she may tuck in her credit card. She crisply and swiftly reaches in her pocket whenever she needs these items. Fumbling is not something an executive woman does.

This shift in where she carries the tools of her trade is one of many little adjustments she has made to subtly enhance the image of her efficiency in the eyes of her male peers.

CONSERVATIVE VERSUS HIGH FASHION

Just how conservatively a woman should dress depends somewhat on the industry she works in.

Conservative Dress Codes	More Relaxed Dress Codes
Aerospace	Advertising
Agricultural equipment	Airlines
Automobiles and Trucking	Apparel/Fashion
Banking and Financial services	Broadcasting/Communications
Brewing	Consumer products
Chemicals	Cosmetics
Computers	Design
Construction/Housing	Filmmaking
Drugs	Food
Electrical equipment	Furniture
Electronics	Hotels
Grocery	Newspapers
Health care	Packaging
Insurance	Publishing
Machinery	Real estate
Maritime	Retailing
Metals	Shoes
Natural resources	Textiles
Transportation	Television
Utilities	

It is important to note that the industries with more relaxed dress codes apply these codes for the most part at the middle and lower management levels. There you may see trendier and brighter dresses, more individual makeup and trendier hairstyles.

Life at the top for the senior woman executive does not vary greatly from the advertising industry to the oil business. Like men at the top, women at the top dress very much alike.

In an industry where dress is more relaxed, however, the executive may make a slightly stronger fashion statement. Her clothes may be a little less classic and slightly more trendy. They are nonetheless subdued and recognizably expensive.

Incidentally, expensive looks are not necessarily expensive. They are classic, timeless, conservative, neat and carefully groomed looks. The executive woman realizes, however, that one good wool tweed skirt is worth four cheaply made unlined polyester skirts. She always forgoes quantity for quality and is careful to make sure that her choice is apparent.

Executive women, regardless of the industry they are in, have a subtle style that sets them apart from the lower- and middle-ranked women in their companies. You would never mistake these poised, immaculately groomed women for their secretaries. Everything the executive wears, carries and does signals authority and success.

EXECUTIVE COLORS

Executive colors have been determined by the colors men wear to the executive suite. Suits are muted gray, navy, brown, tweed or blue. Shirts are white or pale tones. As an executive, a woman appears most powerful wearing these colors. For her most important meetings, the executive woman always wears suits and blouses very similar to choices available in the typical male executive closet.

However, as a woman she does have a somewhat broader range of colors to wear on a day-to-day basis than men have. Deep tones of green or plum are acceptable for suits and blouses. Moreover, brown, black and navy blouses are appropriate on executive women, whereas they are unacceptable for men. The colors red, orange and purple are included in the executive woman's wardrobe on a very limited basis, although white, taupe and ecru are worn often in the summer. No red, orange or purple ever enters the boardroom. When her message is important, she doesn't give men a chance to think how well her lipstick matches her suit. She wants them thinking about her ideas.

EXECUTIVE FABRICS

Fine wools, wool gabardines, and finely finished silks and silk blends are the ideal fabrics for executive suits. Silk is ideal for shirts and blouses.

Cotton is acceptable for blouses if it is finely finished. Ultrasuede may be a staple in the executive woman's wardrobe. Polyester fabrics are acceptable only if nobody will ever guess they are man-made. Knit suits are acceptable if they are obviously expensive and look crocheted. Generally, double knits, polyesters and linens are unacceptable in the executive suite. Knits and polyesters are to be eschewed because they look less expensive—and money means power. Linen is avoided because it wrinkles: The crumpled linen look is far too casual to be worn in a conservative executive office.

Antique handwork and exquisite details on blouses are properly expensive-looking and do have a place in the executive suite.

EXECUTIVE SUITS

Though it seems clichéd, suits are the basic solution to serious office dressing. Simply put, suits are more traditional in the office than even dresses because men have worn suits to work for centuries.

Since secretaries and low-management women have adopted the suit solution, the selection an executive woman makes must be distinctive. Like her male counterparts, she dresses to set herself apart. Her suit is distinguished by the obvious fineness of its cut and fit and the richness of its fabric. She buys it expecting to wear it for ten years. She knows no one can date it by its cut. It is classic.

The skirt is lined and fits loosely enough to survive hours of sitting without being wrinkled.

The executive woman avoids the pat suit look popular with middle management, i.e., the tweed suit worn with a white Peter Pan–collared blouse. She opts for a dressier, more opulent look, relying on rich texture and color to distinguish her. She individualizes her look with carefully chosen accessories.

EXECUTIVE SUIT SUBSTITUTES

The executive woman further varies her suit look by mixing and matching skirts, blouses and jackets. This permits her to get by with a smaller wardrobe. She makes sure that the combination looks carefully coordinated and that the proportions of the jacket and skirt complement each other.

Fine silk blouses lend elegance to combinations. A variety of styles and fabrics softens the routine look of her other clothes.

"For the first three months a woman is at a new job she should wear a suit every day. That establishes a very businesslike presence. Then she can vary her look without diluting her effectiveness," suggests a successful executive.

LENGTH OF EXECUTIVE SKIRTS

The executive's skirts are neither long nor short; they are below her knees, somewhere in the mid- to upper-calf zone. Generally, since she wears a suit for as much as a decade, there is little about a skirt to attract special attention. When she sits, the skirt never rises above her knee. Knees are too sexy to be executive.

EXECUTIVE DRESSES

"Some women used to look like they were going to a cocktail party when they came to the office. I think that's why the pendulum swung to gray flannel suits," observes Dr. Dorothy Gregg. "I think the pendulum has leveled off. Dresses are now okay again."

A banker concurs: "Ten years ago the office look for a woman was more a uniform. The fashion industry has tuned in on the working woman and I think now you can be businesslike and still express your personality."

As long as the dress is simple, high-necked, tailored and elegant, it is appropriate for the boardroom. It must be a solid color or small subdued print.

One woman relates that she wore the wrong dress to the president's office. It was a hot summer day and the dress was sleeveless. "I said 'It's cold in here.' He said, 'That's why you shouldn't wear a dress to work.' I got the message," she recalls.

"If I am going to an office at another company, I always wear a jacket over the dress. I just feel a jacket is more executive," notes Colombe Nicholas.

EXECUTIVE NECKLINES

The best neckline for an executive blouse is around the executive neck, of course. Blouses that wrap up high around the neck are even more effective when women are particularly interested in having men concentrate on what they are saying.

Still, it is acceptable to leave a high-collared blouse unbuttoned at the top. This is particularly effective if the executive wears beautiful pearls that are glimpsed through the opening. This looks even better if she has a golden tan.

Slightly cut-away V-necklines and rounded ones are less businesslike. For an ordinary un-high-powered day at the office, the woman executive may wear a more casual blouse without diluting her image with her staff.

Under no condition does the executive woman ever show any hint of cleavage. She never lets her neckline even approach the vicinity of her bosom. Breasts are feminine. "Feminine" in the male-dominated bastions such as the boardroom means vulnerable/weak.

The executive woman knows she should always stress attributes that are powerful. She knows her face is her most powerful feature, so she dresses in a manner that does not call attention away from it.

SWEATERS ARE NOT EXECUTIVE

Sweaters, unless they are worn under a suit jacket and she is small-busted, have no place in the day-to-day wardrobe of the executive woman. Sweaters are typically perceived as middle management—not executive—and like the sweaters worn by her male counterparts, knitted beauties fit in best on weekends and holidays. If she is not flat-chested, sweaters call attention to the executive bosom.

EXECUTIVE SHOES

The executive woman avoids provocative evening-style sandals as well as flat shoes. If she is on the short side, high heels (about two inches high) enhance her bearing by elevating her to an eye-to-eye stance with taller men. And if she is tall, high heels further capitalize on her height. Height in male terms is powerful. (The "little woman" was not a woman who had any chance of being a powerful business woman.)

Shoes should be beautiful, but never flashy, trendy or so ornate as to call attention to themselves. It is, however, acceptable for the executive to indulge a fine ankle or beautiful foot.

Shoes should be simple and businesslike. "The wrong shoes can undo everything," comments Adelaide Sink, who routinely warns young women to avoid casual shoes.

EXECUTIVE STOCKINGS

The executive always wears stockings to the office, regardless of the temperature. They are sheer and simple. They may be dark and coordinated to her shoes and skirt or they may be skin-colored. Colored, contrasting stockings are not executive enough to make it into the boardroom; ditto opaque and patterned stockings.

Note: Skin-colored stockings have two advantages. They don't show runs and snags, and they go with any outfit so they are one less thing for the busy executive woman to concern herself with.

EXECUTIVE COATS

Down or polyester-filled coats are warm and practical but not executive. They are too casual for the office. Executive women reserve them for their private life. The executive woman wears fur or a classically cut wool coat.

The color is coordinated with what she is wearing underneath: A black coat goes over black and gray, a blue coat over blue, etc. Otherwise she wears a beige coat that goes with everything. Her raincoat is a standard good-quality raincoat indistinguishable from the ones worn by male colleagues.

During the cold season, a fur coat is not essential. Better an elegantly cut cloth coat than a cheap fur. If she wears a fur coat it is mink, raccoon or fox.

EXECUTIVE HATS

Hats have no more place in the office for the executive woman than for her male counterparts. If it is cold or rainy she can wear a hat out-of-doors with her coat. Generally speaking, she will never be seen wearing a hat if no man around is wearing one. Wearing a hat indoors or to lunch is too feminine. Her male peers are already well aware of her gender.

EXECUTIVE GLOVES

Mittens and knitted gloves are frivolous. Executive gloves are kid, lined with polyester or silk in temperate climates and with wool in cold places. They are a dark color.

EXECUTIVE SCARVES

One of the accessories an executive relies on to vary her office uniform is a scarf. It is obviously fine and printed heavy silk, and is usually recognizable to other executives as Hermes or Gucci or something similarly familiar. Under no circumstances does she wear the scarf with its identification showing. Since its expensive origins are immediately recognized by her peers, she knots it in such a way that the signature is concealed. Since she's made it to the top, she doesn't need to advertise that she shops at the best places.

A colorful scarf provides a simple, soft touch that relieves the elegant grimness of her suits without diluting her professional image.

THE EXECUTIVE BRIEFCASE

The executive woman carries a classic unisex briefcase, made of leather or canvas. It is of excellent quality and indeterminate origin. "Indeterminate origin" means that there are no initials or designer stripes or fittings to indicate who produced it. The opening can be accessed without turning the briefcase sideways: She can hold the briefcase with one hand and reach in with the other rather than having to set it down on its side and open it with two hands.

A shoulder strap is a great asset if she travels because it leaves her hands free to carry her luggage. But she avoids wearing a shoulder strap routinely to the office, since it blurs the distinction between purse and briefcase. The strap is detachable so it can be stored when its use is not absolutely essential. Men automatically recognize a briefcase when it is carried in the hand.

At times the executive woman may opt for carrying a tote holding her papers and a small purse to the office. If she is planning on shopping for personal household items at lunch, she appears more professional carrying a tote than she would returning with assorted paper bags. The tote is canvas or leather and like the briefcase is unmarked, unless it has the emblem of an art museum or other publicly supported institution.

EXECUTIVE PURSES

If her male colleagues are carrying briefcases, the executive woman carries a briefcase. No purse.

When she goes to lunch and the men do not carry briefcases, it is then appropriate for her to carry a small, unobtrusive clutch or bag (if her pockets are not adequate to carry her lipstick, cards, pen and credit cards and money.) The bag should be small, classic, and expensive-looking. It should reinforce her image if someone focuses on it, but it is not conspicuous.

Some women carry small, flat clutches in their briefcases all ready to go to lunch just in case the committee huddles around a lunch club table.

EXECUTIVE COUNTRY LOOK

Country tweedy clothes are very attractive but have no place in the executive suite in an industry that encourages conservative dressing. Unless she works on the West Coast or in an industry noted for its relaxed dress codes, the executive woman reserves her fringed suede confections, cashmere sweaters, tweedy suits and boots for her private life. She does, however, wear them to corporate meetings at the hunting lodge on Saturday afternoon or on a Sunday afternoon at the boss's country house. A dressier look is generally more powerful.

EXECUTIVE PANTS

Many men are threatened by women in pantsuits. They regard pantsuits as too butch. Therefore, skirts are more universally appropriate, since the point of executive dressing is to create a positive presence.

In more casual industries or on days when she is tending to routine, low-visibility business, the executive woman may opt to wear a gracious, preferably pleated, lined pair of pants to the office.

If she has a large behind, pants are an absolute no-no. Generally, no one larger than a size eight should wear pants.

EXECUTIVE HAIRSTYLES

Executive hair is controlled, shiny and clean, and obviously well cared for. It is styled well *off* the face, not on the face. Faces are powerful. Hair is feminine.

Nor is hair frizzy. Frizzy is cute. Cute is not executive. Long hair sweeping over the shoulders is sexy—not executive. If longer than shoulder length, hair should be worn in a bun at the nape of the neck or tidily arranged on the back or top of the head. Long hair down the back is for the executive woman's private life, not her corporate life. The men she works with cannot imagine what her private life is like. Or if she has one.

Any pins or combs are simple and expensive.

Hair is best worn shorter than shoulder length and styled very simply. Most executive women opt for short hair, which they wash every morning and blow-dry themselves. "I cut my hair because it was just one more hassle in my life," says the president of a New York company.

EXECUTIVE LIPSTICK

A woman is more conspicuous without lipstick than she is with it. Therefore she should wear it, but carefully. The color is never in any way startling. Executives wear lipsticks that are in themselves never singled out. Middle-range pinks and reds are usual staples. Fuchias, white and conspicuously frosted lipsticks are out.

A firm color base applied with a lipstick pencil is durable and maintains a consistent color through a long day. Lipstick can be easily concealed in a woman's pockets and reapplied during meeting breaks. By keeping it fresh discreetly, she calls no attention to it. She has spare lipsticks in many different places.

EXECUTIVE MAKEUP

Generally, the executive's cosmetics are contained in a small leather or canvas bag in her briefcase. This bag should be unmarked with flowers or any cute decoration and absolutely unidentifiable to any male colleague who might spy it. It generally contains a mirror, lipstick, tissue and comb. The executive woman is prepared to look fresh every day. Virtually every executive woman in America has at least a lipstick and a comb secreted in her briefcase at all times.

Whether she wears makeup or not is unimportant; what is important is that she is absolutely consistent. She either never wears makeup or is always perfectly made up. It is not executive to startle her colleagues. If she wears makeup it is always kept absolutely consistent through any working time period. It is never allowed to be smudged or smeared and is always kept fresh-looking. This is easy since it was applied to last for eighteen hours.

If an executive uses makeup, she uses it artfully. Makeup should embellish, not detract, and may also make a subtle statement about the nature of the industry in which she is involved.

An advertising or fashion executive may wear fully applied foundation, mascara, liner, eyeshadow and lipstick. She might complete her statement about who she is with her jewelry and her fashionably cut suit. Her counterpart at a staid computer or financial company might restrict her makeup to foundation, blush and lipstick. By the same token, she would wear an expensive, beautifully made suit of less obviously fashionable design that she had made in England five years ago.

Under no circumstances does the executive wear iridescent eye makeup, heavy eyeliner or gold-flecked blush. Those are associated all too quickly with women who are markedly uninterested in getting ahead.

Any makeup the executive woman wears is not only harmonious but also very contemporary. Chances are she consults yearly with the makeup specialist at her hairdresser's salon. Regular updates assure that she won't get trapped with an outmoded look which could make her appear dated and older than she actually is. Looking out-of-date would undermine her effectiveness with young junior managers.

EXECUTIVE MIRRORS

The executive woman is concerned about her appearance but she certainly does not want her vanity to be apparent to her peers. (Vanity is interpreted as a weakness.) Yet the effectiveness of the woman executive is enhanced if her appearance is always exactly as she intends.

She has mirrors, but in private places. For instance, she keeps a small mirror in a pocket of her briefcase so she can check herself whenever she has even a thirty-second interlude. Nobody knows. If she has a wall cabinet with a door in her office, she might place a mirror on the inside of the door. One flick and she can check herself on her way into an important meeting. If she has no doored cabinets, she might place a small mirror at eye level under the coat hook on the back of her office door where her coat will cover it.

She tells her associate that she has "one more call to make quickly before I join you" and freshens up in her office before entering a session that is long or important.

One reason an executive woman may freshen up in her office instead of the company rest room is that there is no executive washroom for women. Therefore, her personal grooming must be performed to the fascination of the female switchboard operator or her own female secretary. Junior women are as interested in executives as are junior men—which is why male executives invented the executive washroom. A woman executive is no happier than her male counterparts in having her personal toilet reported on to her underlings. But typically she has no private washroom to retreat to. Frequently there is only one executive toilet—for men only.

EXECUTIVE NAILS

A woman's hands are an important part of her business presence, since she spends most of her time seated at desks and tabletops with her hands between her and her male associates.

Executive hands are obviously well cared for. The nails are medium length and polished a shade of red. They look unchipped and freshly manicured. Cared-for, well-manicured, painted nails connote leisure and good life-support systems. Successful women indicate that they have these (even if they have to do their own nails at midnight).

Typically, executives do their nails themselves on the weekends.

Very long nails, chipped polish, purple polish, or clear nail polish and short nails should not be found on the executive woman.

EXECUTIVE PERFUME

The executive woman knows it is fine and well to remind a man that she is a woman when she is in the bedroom. But in the boardroom? Forget it! She doesn't need to remind anyone. She ignores heavy perfume and scent. These are not part of her public life.

EXECUTIVE TANS

Having a light suntan is an excellent cosmetic. If a woman is tanned a good part of the year it not only looks pretty but also suggests that she spends her leisure time playing a lot of tennis or some other outdoor sports. This in turn implies that she is so successful that she has reached a point where she does not have to slave at her office seven days a week.

EXECUTIVE WEIGHT

The executive woman is not overweight. If she had extra pounds, she lost them. Being slim and fit makes her feel better as well as look better. It says that she not only values her contribution, she values herself and thus takes good care of herself. Executives are slim and fit.

"There's no question there's a double standard about women's weight. If they weigh fifteen pounds too much, it's used against them. Leanness is in. Executive is lean," comments an industrial executive. She works out at a nearby cardiovascular center.

To conclude, remember that *the following things are never seen on the executive woman:*

- Cleavage
- Heavy perfume
- Tight sweaters
- Tight pants
- Teetering evening sandals
- Slit skirts
- Rumpled linen skirts and tops
- Bows in the hair
- Cute bangs
- Frizzy-permed hair
- Very long nails
- Short bitten nails
- Mittens
- Seamed stockings
- Purple nail polish
- Bulging stomach in a tight skirt
- Drip-dry suits

5 BUZZ WORDS
AND THE
BOARDROOM

The woman who has made it to the top in American business knows the right buzz words to turn on her male colleagues and impress the bankers she deals with. She uses these words generously to help make the point that she is a serious and savvy executive, something she might not be perceived as were she not to use them.

Many of the buzz words are financially oriented, and there's a simple reason for this. Men love to talk about money because with money comes power. "There is more talk in the boardroom about money than sports and sex," reports one awed executive. "What men really love to talk about is money, money, money."

The successful woman may not have studied finance or economics in college, but she has learned basic concepts and phrases on the job. Though some women have been intimidated by finance classes in school, the concepts are so fundamental that they are picked up on the job effortlessly.

If a woman does not have the opportunity to learn basic accounting and finance on her job, she teaches herself by reading the *Wall Street Journal* every day and asking questions about unfamiliar phrases—if there is someone she trusts enough to reveal her ignorance. Otherwise she takes an evening course at a local college. She also attends the seminars provided at no charge by the major brokerage firms.

Knowing the right phrases can give a woman an important advantage. "Men can't believe it when a woman understands money. At first they are amazed. Then they include you," reports a vice president.

"Don't stop with the vocabulary. The words are the beginning point. Use all the right words, but you've also got to integrate finance into your thinking," remarks Judith Moncrieff, an executive in the public affairs office of Mobile Corporation, a company larger than many countries. She learned more about business on the job than she did in the classroom. "Financial concepts are essential in your understanding of a corporation's priorities," she claims.

Moreover, the buzz words you hear used most frequently reveal the priorities of top management.

EXECUTIVE BUZZ WORDS AND CONCEPTS

Adjusted earnings after inflation. This refers to how much money a person (or a corporation) actually has to spend after inflation has been factored into her earnings. In figuring how much of an increase in buying power she has, the executive first is careful to deduct the percentage of inflation for a given period from the percentage of increase of the income. "When I adjust my earnings to inflation I find I have less money than I had a decade or a year ago," is a familiar lament in the executive corridors.

"Inflation-adjusted" dollars are sometimes referred to as "constant dollars" or "real dollars."

When she's negotiating a raise, the successful woman talks about "real dollars."

Affordable. Whether to refer to her division's overhead or to her personal affairs, the woman executive uses this word to indicate that monetary considerations have been given to the subject.

After-tax earnings. This refers to how much money the executive actually has on hand after taxes since, after all, money that Uncle Sam takes from her does not buy her anything. It also applies to how much money companies make after they pay their taxes. If the amount a company "nets" (makes) seems high, it is good to ask if that figure is "after taxes." Often companies pay almost half their profits in taxes.

Annual report. This is a report issued by law by all companies whose stock is traded by the public. If this document is issued by the company an executive works for or by those she deals with, she studies it carefully. This booklet, issued annually, updates each sector of the company's business and gives an official statement as to its past and future performance. It is a treasure trove of information about the company. The executive woman understands it, either on her own, through a course offered by a local college, or with the help of an accountant.

Assets. These are any of the things a person (or company) has that are of any value. They can include anything from cash, property, patents and equipment, to industrial production facilities (commonly referred to as "plants").

Asset rich, cash poor. This means that she (or a company) has lots of holdings but for whatever reason has decided not to cash them in right now. Thus, she does not have a great deal of ready cash. This is a nice way of saying she's broke but not poor. "Rich on paper" is another way of talking about assets in contrast to cash. It also implies substantial assets but little cash.

Even if she is really poor, the executive woman does not casually admit it. Saying "I'm cash poor right now" or "I'm suffering a cash flow dilemma" is honest—but less revealing.

Asset redeployment. When assets, usually corporate assets, are redeployed, they have been sold for cash. Consequently, that cash was reinvested to purchase something else. "Deployment" is one of those words with military overtones favored by the male business community. Militarily, it means spreading out troops according to a plan to cover a broader area. It's the implication of having a strategy that makes this a favorite corporate phrase.

Benchmark. This means an important point of reference. The term comes from the jargon of surveyors, who would take an object already known as a reference point to measure tides and other variables. Whenever an important ruling is issued by a federal agency, it becomes a benchmark for the affected industries.

Big ticket item. This refers to the price tag on an object. A high price is a big ticket. This is a slang phrase that indicates a familiarity with money matters. "After all, a new computer is a big ticket item," an executive might say to an underling who has suggested some major equipment purchases.

Bottom line. "Give me the bottom line" means "Tell me what the ultimate results are plain and simple, without any details. Do we make money or don't we?" The bottom line refers to the final line listed in corporate financial statements. Traditionally, it tells, after all is said and done and taxes are paid and losses are absorbed, how much money was made or lost. If the bottom line is zilch, is the project worth taking on?

Buy low, sell high. This refers to the basis of capitalism, buying cheaply and selling when you can get a great deal more.

Capital. This refers to cash on hand. "The company has little available capital to spend" means the company does not have much cash. A "capital expenditure" is an amount of money spent to improve existing equipment or facilities or to buy or build new ones. It is usually a substantial amount of money.

Capital gains. This refers to a tax law that permits the taxes paid on profits from selling assets held for a certain length of time to be less than the taxes generally levied on ordinary income of corporations or individuals. This law encourages some stability in the real estate and stock markets by providing an incentive for many investors to hold investments longer than they might otherwise.

CEO and COO. The abbreviations for chief executive officer, the head honcho of a company, and the chief operating officer, the number two person in corporate hierarchy. Using the initials makes a woman appear familiar with top responsibilities. Traditionally, the CEO is concerned with corporate and industry direction and takes an overview of the business, while the COO is concerned with the day-to-day business of a company. Frequently, the COO is the only person to report to the CEO, while many people report to the COO. Usually, although not always, the CEO is the chairman of the board and the COO is the president of the company. Sometimes one person is CEO, chairman and president, and there is no COO.

Chapter 11. A company that is going into Chapter 11 is on the verge of bankruptcy. Chapter 11 is a part of the Federal Bankruptcy Code that protects a company from its creditors while it reorganizes. The company continues to operate, although usually the court appoints other management to sort out its affairs.

Closely held companies. The stock of these firms is controlled by a few people. These companies may or may not be publicly held.

Commodity. In the business pages, this usually refers to an agricultural or mine product. Guesses or estimates as to future prices ("futures") are traded on various national commodity exchanges. Trading commodity futures is a tricky business best left to professional traders. Some of the commodities that are traded are corn, soybeans, wheat, cattle, pork bellies, cocoa, cotton, coffee, orange juice, sugar, copper, gold, silver, heating oil, lumber and plywood.

Common stock. There is no "uncommon stock." Most shares of stock that are traded in the stock market are common stock. When people mention "stock" they are usually referring to what is more technically known as common stock.

Contrarian. "After all, I'm a contrarian at heart." When a woman says this she means she first listens to what the mainstream is advising, then marches to the beat of her own drummer. This implies that she has a mind of her own and that she is willing to take risks, since in her view most of the people are wrong most of the time. Her theory is that if everybody is doing it it must be time to do something else.

If she is proven to be right much of the time—and she wouldn't be where she is if she had not been right on important occasions—this attests to her intelligence. It also underscores her self-confidence without her needing to brag.

Cost savings. Any good executive cuts her costs whenever and wherever she can. The subject is a popular one in the executive suite, whether the outcome is positive or negative. Making the statement, "That's not a real cost savings," indicates that an executive is not impressed by a simplistic approach to cutting costs because she is aware that other, less obvious costs exist. Once again, this makes her appear savvy.

Cyclicals. Sometimes called cyclical industries, these businesses are recognized to have wide swings in performance, based on the economic climate. Some cyclical industries are steel, mining, railroads, autos, paper, chemicals, rubber, construction, furniture, textiles and major appliances. No matter how wonderful the management of a company in one of these industries may be, the company is unlikely to be able to sustain a consistent growth record. This means it experiences periodic layoffs, shutdowns and cutbacks.

Debt service. This is the amount of interest that has to be paid regularly on money that has been borrowed. "That company is not making a profit because its debt service is killing it" refers to a company which is so indebted for money it has previously borrowed that it has difficulty generating enough profit to offset that cost, much less to make an additional profit.

In the early eighties, when borrowed money carried interest rates of 15 percent to 20 percent some cash-desperate companies incurred terrible burdens. One hundred thousand dollars borrowed at 20 percent means a company has to repay $20,000 the first year—that's before it has repaid a cent of the principal. (It probably has three to five years to repay its total debt.)

Discount brokers. These are "no-frills" brokerage firms that will buy or sell stock for much less than the brokerage firms which are household words. On a trade of $5,000, you can save about 50 percent of the typical brokerage commission. On anything less, you save virtually nothing. On more than $5,000, you save more than fifty percent. They give you no advice, no sales pitch and no fancy literature and seminars. How much is charged varies from one firm to the next.

Dividend. When the executive uses this term, she is referring to the amount of money paid out regularly from the earnings of a company to the people who own shares of its stock. A dividend is paid out on a per share basis.

Down cycle. This is a euphemistic phrase to indicate that business is bad but it is expected to be good. By saying, "Right now we're in a down cycle," the executive implies her familiarity with the business phases of certain industries, such as chemicals and housing. They have traditionally had wide cyclic swings in performance. "Up cycle" implies business is good but it has been, and is likely to be again in the future, bad.

Equity. In business, this refers to common stock. Having equity means owning a piece of the pie.

Equity markets. This refers to the stock and bond markets. The major markets are the New York Stock Exchange, The American Stock Exchange and the Over-the-Counter market.

Executive. This is a word used more outside the executive suite than within. "Senior management" is preferred by executives to describe themselves.

Fiscal year. An American organization can choose any twelve months for its accounting system. If those twelve months are not from January 1 through December 31, its fiscal year is not the same as the calendar year.

The U.S. government has a fiscal year that runs from July 1 through June 30. Changing the fiscal year from one period to another is quite complicated.

Gold. When investors talk about gold, they usually are speaking of gold coins or bars of gold buillion. The price of gold is determined solely by current market demand. Numismatics is concerned solely with gold coins, which are valued not only by the price of gold but also by rarity, beauty, and other variables.

Gross revenues. This is the total amount of sales before the costs of producing the goods or doing business are deducted. Net revenues is the figure after the costs of returns, spoilage, etc., are deducted.

Institutions. This refers to banks and various money funds in financial circles. Everything not individual is institutional.

Liabilities. These are any debts the company has that have to be paid, even if they are long-term debts not payable for twenty years. A liability is any outstanding debt.

Loss carry-forward. This basically is a tax-related term which means that money lost in one period gives the company a tax concession in some future period. Generally speaking, it is better for an executive not to cause a loss. But if she does, the loss carry-forward aspect is one positive factor that can mitigate the actual impact of the loss.

Market share. This is a popular phrase in industries having to do with consumer products or the public at large. "What share of the market does XYZ have?" is a question the executive will ask a consumer products or broadcasting executive for openers when she is making small talk. This phrase is a major buzz word in some businesses.

Money managers. These people are paid to invest money for institutions and investors. They may "run" the money of a pension fund or mutual fund or they may "run" the cash of a financial institution. "Running money" means investing it on a large scale.

Municipals. These are the bonds issued by cities, counties and states. They usually yield a lower return than corporate bonds but give investors an offsetting tax break.

One-time expenditure. This describes something expensive initially but worth the price when its long-term profitability is analyzed.

Output. This has to do with the amount of work done over any particular period. Productivity in factories and plants is sometimes measured by output.

P/e multiple. This is the ratio of the price of the stock of a corporation to the earnings per share earned by the company in a given period. "P" stands for price and "e" stands for earnings. A high multiple (30 and above) may indicate that the company earned little during its last reporting period but investors feel things will improve. Or it may mean that major investors have followed each other like lemmings to buy the stock and have bid its price up past all reason.

Parley. This is a formal conference that may include a series of discussions and negotiations.

Perks. This is short for perquisite, and the executive woman rarely uses the term unless she's acknowledging one to a colleague. "A limousine to and from the airport is one of the nice perks they give me," she smiles graciously. Perks are an important part of her compensation, since they are services, memberships and privileges that are not technically her salary and go largely untaxed. Lunch clubs, company cars, country club memberships and liberal free use of her expense account are only a few perks she gets. To provide them herself out of her own earnings, after tax, of course would be costly indeed. Moreover, these nice benefits make a powerful statement about her status, position and value. They impress her peers. That favorable impression can be precious indeed when she is soliciting an ally to support her in an upcoming position or appointment.

Pitfalls. This is used to describe all the things that can go wrong. The executive woman never says, "This project scares the daylights out of me." She says calmly, "This project contains many pitfalls." If she's terrified, she says the project is "fraught with peril."

Portfolio. This is the total array of investments held by an individual. It includes cash, stocks, real estate and other assets.

Profitability. This is a key word. Enhanced profitability and increased productivity are the goal of the key executive. She stresses profitability to her peers every step of the way. Increasing profitability is one way she wins respect in the male business community.

Public versus private. Public companies are those that have shares traded among the general public. Private companies are those that have never offered any shares for public sale.

R & D. The savvy way to refer to research and development.

Return on investment (sometimes called simply ROI). This is the amount of profit an executive earns for every dollar spent. If she invests $1 and receives 20 cents, her rate of return is 20 percent.

Revenues versus profits. Revenues are how much money was brought in. Profits are how much money, after all the costs and overhead taxes are paid, was actually made. An executive knows it is more important to increase profits than sales.

S & L's. The savvy way to refer to savings and loan institutions.

Senior personnel. This is used to refer not to age but to position. It describes the executives as distinct from the other employees. To be the most senior is to be the top-ranked.

Setback. The executive woman has learned not to call "disasters," "failures" and "mistakes" by those words—particularly if she was in any way involved. She calls them setbacks. This implies forward motion is taking place, just not from as forward a position as previously.

Smokestack industries. So named because of the smokestacks that used to burn coal to power them, these are the heavy industries that were America's backbone during the first half of the twentieth century. Their importance is on the decline as business shifts to high technology and service-oriented companies such as communications.

Some smokestack businesses:
- Aluminum
- Automotive
- Chemicals
- Machinery
- Steel
- Utilities

Software. This is opposed to hardware, which is physical equipment. Software generally refers to computer programming.

Solely owned. Refers to a company held entirely by one owner. If that owner is a person, the company is private. If that owner is a publicly held company, then the company is a subsidiary.

Start-up costs. The executive uses this term when she is in favor of a project that is expensive but that she believes will prove ultimately profitable. This phrase is used to refer to the initial shortfall between revenues generated by the new project and the costs of starting it.

Strategic plan. This is redundant, since a strategy is a plan, but the executive has learned that men in the executive suite respond favorably to war words. Strategy reminds them of war plans and readiness, as in the Strategic Air Command.

Thrifts. This is another way savings and loan banks are referred to in the financial pages.

Undervalued. Stocks of a company that many observers may find particularly cheap are called undervalued. Whether they are in fact undervalued is never certain.

Unnecessary expenditures. This phrase is used to castigate a project or a manager. Wasting money goes against the objectives of a profit-making business. Money is to be conserved and spent wisely and constructively. A corporation, unlike the Congress, cannot print money as needed. To spend it unnecessarily is to sin.

Viable. This and "feasible" are two favorite words used in the boardroom in lieu of "practicable" or "doable." Said slowly, the word implies deep consideration is being given to something.

Vice president. This means different things in different companies. In some it is a title held by literally thousands. Banks and service companies seem to have the most. Banks have first, second, third, senior and group vice presidents. On the other hand, some companies have a handful of vice presidents, each of whom is genuinely important. A vice president who is important reports to the president. Otherwise, the top level is the one that does report directly to the chief operating officer. "Whom do you report to?" is the first question to ask a v.p. to ascertain her importance.

A vice president is a corporate officer, by definition. Whether she also sits on the board of directors is a wholly separate matter. Since top priorities and policies of companies are ultimately determined by their boards of directors, the truly powerful women are both officers and directors.

War-related words. Men have brought the words of war into the corporate battlefield. These words are powerful because they are backed with the explosive content of warfare.

Since many men spend time early on in their youth exposed to military life, it is only natural that the language would continue with them in the corporate world. Moreover, little boys traditionally have been given war toys to play with, so the terminology comes to them more naturally than to women, who played house with their dolls.

Successful women recognize the punch and power that these words carry. They frequently sprinkle them into their conversations and presentation.

- Armed to the teeth—Prepared to take on the opposition.
- Bastion—A fortification; a successfully defended place.
- Battle—A major competition.
- Bomb, bombshell—a stunning revelation.
- Bomb out—To devastate, to be devastated.
- Bombard—To attack with explosive and damaging ammunition.
- Bloodied but unbowed—Vulnerable and somewhat wounded but not out of the game yet.
- D-day—The day a major campaign or undertaking begins.
- Ducking the mortar—Mortar is a type of cannon. During the battle, mortars are fired by opposing sides.
- Taking (or giving) a lot of flak—Flak was fired from World War II anti-aircraft guns. Taking flak means you are under fire, being attacked—usually verbally in the corporate scene.
- Protecting our flanks—Flanks are the outer edges of a battle formation. In business, this generally means you are armed with a contingency plan, leaving no aspect vulnerable to competition.
- Rank and file—This refers to enlisted men and women as opposed to officers. In the corporate arena it refers to the average non-management worker.
- Scrimmage—A small adversarial encounter. The line of scrimmage in sports also has the same military origin.
- Shell-shocked—Reeling from a recent attack. Suggests paralysis.
- Stalemate—A deadlock. Neither adversary has been able to gain the advantage.
- Skirmish—A small encounter, similar to scrimmage. Not the main battle but a small attack away from the main fray.

- Shooting straight—This means someone is being honest and on the level.
- Shooting match—An argument that is settled with deadly information and corporate death blows. A "death blow" is a move that "kills" a corporation, by taking it over or putting it out of business.
- Shoot your way to the top—To gain access to the highest level of a corporation by using your killer instinct and stepping over the bodies. This is vicious corporate gamesmanship.
- Snafu—An acronym for "Situation normal, all fouled up"
- Tactics—Similar to strategy. A strong word that implies a master plan.
- War—All the stops are pulled. Both sides are giving their best energy to competition.
- Warroom—In the military, the key charts are kept here. Whenever a conference room or research room is filled with information, it can be referred to as the warroom.

Widget. Widget is a nonsense word used in business school classes to refer to any given small product that is mass-produced. It is a term used when the point to be made is general and there is no need to be specific.

A widget factory is any factory that produces masses of devices. Hence, tires, tin cans, staplers, and pencils are all produced at widget factories.

COMMONLY DISCUSSED POLITICAL/MONETARY CONCEPTS

The executive woman's world is broader than corporate finance, budgeting and accounting. As she travels among the most important men in the world, she is expected to be knowledgeable about other political and monetary affairs. There is no college course offered in these concepts. She considers it part of her job to be aware of the world and alert to its possibilities and problems.

She reads weekly news magazines and daily newspapers. She considers women's magazines and fashion magazines as "luxury reading" to which she assigns a low priority. If she has free time to read, she probably reads about business and history, since that is what her male peers are likely to be reading. She reads local papers when she travels. Moreover, she is able to discuss broader concepts such as the following:

Cartels. These are monopoly-oriented associations between members who share common goals. A decade ago, OPEC brought the concept of the cartel to the forefront of the economic world when its members organized and agreed to drive up the price of crude petroleum. That particular association wreaked havoc with the economy of all countries dependent on that cartel for oil. Because of OPEC, world leaders cast an increasingly wary eye on attempts by countries, basically Third World members, to unite and drive up the price of any given essential commodity that is in limited supply.

Common Market. This is an economic coalition of European countries. The members give each other certain favorable trade arrangements. Collectively, the nations are sometimes referred to as the European Economic Community (EEC).

Domestic versus cottage industries. "Domestic" refers to goods and industries of a specific country. All U. S.–produced goods are our domestic goods. All of Canada's internally produced goods are her domestic goods. In cottage industries goods are produced in households and then delivered to a central business point. Thus, weaving is a cottage industry in Ireland.

Expansionary credit policy. Some countries, such as the U. S., decide to buy more goods from foreign countries than they can pay for. They import now and hope to pay later. It is a controversial move, objected to by countries that try harder to live within their current means.

Glut. A glut occurs when a product is available far in excess of demand. Prices drop. This is a favorite topic of conversation when it occurs because it has a major negative impact on the surrounding economy. Thus, when we have a grain glut, the farmers make less, cannot afford farm equipment, and so that sector suffers too. When we have a copper glut, South American economies reel under the effect and have trouble repaying their debts to the U.S.

Gross National Product (GNP). This is the total dollar amount of business done within a country during any given period of time. In a recession, less business is done, so the GNP shrinks. In a healthy economy the opposite is true. An "expanding economy" is a happy subject of conversation.

International Monetary Fund (IMF). This is a system supported by richer developed countries to loan money to underdeveloped countries who have problems with paying their bills. It bails them out for the short haul so they can hopefully recover and get their act together for the long haul. It also provides other sophisticated financial services.

International monetary system. This usually refers to the international network of various currencies and their relationship to each other. When too much borrowing occurs by an important country or by several countries from other countries the monetary system becomes unbalanced.

Multinational versus international. This is a sophisticated distinction used to differentiate companies that have operations in several countries from companies that not only have operations in several countries but routinely think in global terms. Thus a company such as Coca Cola is a truly international country because it thinks in terms of having its product consumed everywhere. A semiconductor firm that has a manufacturing operation in the Far East but is thinking in terms of the American market is merely multinational. There is more status in the business community for the international planner and business person than the multinational.

Protectionism. This is a sensitive issue with countries outside of the U.S. who fear that they will be restricted from the world's richest consumer market. Protectionism means that to protect our domestically produced goods we tax imported competitive goods so heavily they are unattractive to U. S. consumers. This means that other countries cannot realistically compete in the U.S.

Third World countries. Technically, these countries are limited to African and Asian countries that are neutral on communism. The term is often used more generally to include all the underdeveloped countries on earth. Economists frequently refer to these countries as "UDCs."

SPORTS AND THE BOARDROOM

The executive woman long ago learned that sports moved from the college football team and the Sunday television set right into the boardroom. "Sometimes in the mornings after a major game on television the night before we talk about the sports almost as much as we discuss the business at hand," notes a woman who is frequently the only female present. If she is over fifty years of age, chances are that while the boys were out playing football she was going to ballet and piano. If she is under fifty chances are she played tennis—not baseball or football, the two most influential sports in corporate vocabularies.

But that has not slowed her corporate progress. The executive knows her male colleagues respond positively to the sports jargon they have imported to the executive planning committee. Even though she didn't grow up on the playing field, she can hold her own bandying the sports terminology in the boardroom. "It's healthy to have at least a rudimentary knowledge of major sports and major athletes. You can't sit there all the time while the guys discuss sports and not know what they're talking about or express an opinion," declares Mary Jane Raphael, an ABC executive who is in her mid-thirties and a golfer herself.

She relies on sports terminology to add strength—and punch—to her presentations. She talks about "close calls," asks for "time out" (complete with hand signal), "keeps score" and "makes points." Being executive means she communicates effectively. Since sports talk, she talks sports.

BALL

Many business phrases involve the use of the word "ball," the center of many a sport.
• "Run with the ball."—This is a phrase used when a project has been given a green light to proceed. To run with the ball implies eagerness.
• "The ball is in your court."—This tells someone the onus is on her (or him) to take action.

- "You've got the ball."—This underscores the responsibility held by someone for a project.
- To "have something on the ball"—To be quick-witted and smart.
- "Get the ball rolling."—This refers to beginning an undertaking. It indicates eagerness to begin.
- "Play Ball"—To begin.

GAMES

Games are in high favor in the corporate suite. The executive woman views herself as a skilled player.
- "Name of the game"—This is usually bad news, e.g. "The name of the game is dirty tricks."
- "Fair game"—Available to the most skilled player. A legitimate target.
- "Ahead of the game"—One step ahead of the competition.
- "Make game of"—To ridicule someone or something.
- "Play the game by the rules"—Someone who doesn't is playing dirty, being dishonest or violating a code of honor.
- "The game is up."—The game is over. Usually said if the game has been lost.
- "Plays one's game well"—To gain respect for how one played.
- "Game plan"—The plan of action to achieve a certain goal.

PLAYING

Games are *played*. Playing has made its way into corporate jargon.
- "Play up to"—To curry favor.
- "Play for time"—To delay in hopes of gaining an advantage in what is otherwise a losing proposition.
- "Playing around"—This refers to nonproductive activity. "Let's stop playing around and get down to work."
- "Play out"—To see a project to its conclusion.
- "Play both ends against the middle"—To expand one's options to enhance the chances of winning. This is similar to backing several horses in the same race.
- "Play with the big boys"—To play in the big league. The stakes are high. The game is money. The winner takes all.

SPORTS

Words specifically referring to sports have also crept into business vocabularies. Sports, like games, are team efforts to achieve clearly stated goals.
- "Being a sport"—This means being amicable and easygoing.

• "Make sport of"—This means not taking a topic or person seriously.
• "A good sport"—This is the person who hangs in the game and plays by the rules.

BASEBALL AND FOOTBALL

Some words have come to business from baseball and football, the two most popular American games.

• "Ballpark figure"—This is an approximate quote. If an executive gives a ballpark figure, she has flexibility in revising it slightly higher or lower. If the final figure is close to her original estimate, it's "in the ballpark."

• "Out of left field"—Describes an unexpected move that catches the executive off guard. She may miss the ball.

• "Designated hitter"—The person who has been assigned a certain task. If a problem comes along while she's "up at bat"—it's her problem to cope with it.

• "Fumble the ball," "drop the ball"—To fail to accomplish one's assigned task. This slows the progress of the entire team and results in loss of face.

• "Go into a huddle"—Said of the management team when it meets to adjust their game plan.

CASINO GAMES

Words from games in the casino are also used in business.

• "High stakes"—Much money is on the line with the failure or success of a certain venture.

• "Crap game"—A situation in which the variables are out of the players' control. Sometimes expressed as "It depends on the roll of the dice."

• "Play one's cards well"—Negotiate according to a well-thought-out strategy.

• "Play one's cards close to the vest"—Be secretive about one's private game plan.

• "An ace up one's sleeve"—A negotiating variable that is pulled out at a critical moment to win the game.

• "To play an ace"—To use one's most effective ploy. If this doesn't win the goal for the player, he or she probably has lost.

• "Winning streak"—If an executive has been on one of these she has been very, very lucky. Unfortunately, losing streaks also occur.

There are many more phrases, some relating to specific sports, such as "par for the course," which comes from golf and refers to normal problems besetting a project. "Win by a nose" made it to the boardroom from the racetrack, and "lightweight" made it from the boxing ring.

KNOWING THE SCORE

The successful corporate woman studies the daily sports pages and subscribes to a national sports periodical. When she meets Joe Blow, the plant manager in Paducah, she can talk about the pro football game that was televised on the East Coast on the previous Sunday afternoon. She knows that since there is no pro team near him, he is probably going to ask her about her Chicago home town team. She is prepared to discuss many details about the Chicago Cubs. If she wants to "cover all her bases," she has opinions about who else in the league played well last Sunday, how effective the team managers are, and whether the team got its moneys worth in the last trade. Moreover, just in case he's a football or ice hockey diehard, she's sure to have basic and current information about those local teams and their prospects for the upcoming season. She may even have the names of her favorite players on the tip of her tongue, along with her favorite plays from the previous year.

"At first plant managers are uptight because I'm a woman," observes one top industrial executive. "I know that I'm at a disadvantage. But I take it as a challenge. By the time I've made sports talk and small talk through lunch I've usually won them over."

The corporate woman finds that her awareness of sports is an asset in her home office, too. She supports a particular team and most of her male colleagues are aware of it. One way she keeps a high sports profile is by buying season tickets to the games of a particular team. When business obligations interfere, she asks someone whose attention she wants to rouse if he would like to use them. "Sports tickets beat out symphony tickets in a minute," observes one executive, who in her private life secretly prefers the symphony.

Making small wagers on the outcome of pending games is another way to underscore one's sports awareness.

Moreover, the executive woman plays at least one sport and one game. She picks her sport not only because she enjoys it but because it fits her image. There are many she rejects out of hand.

Sports Perceived as Too Weak

Badminton	Frisbee	Shuffleboard
Croquet	Softball	Lawn Bowling
Canasta		

Sports Perceived as Too Mundane/Boring

Rollerskating	Darts	Bowling
Bridge	Rowing	Surfing
Dominoes	Ping-Pong	

Sports Perceived as Too Macho (Aggressive)

Arm wrestling	Wrestling	Weight lifting
Busting broncos	Touch football	Big game hunting
Hockey	Volleyball	Water polo
Billiards	Parachuting	Hang gliding
Motorcycling	Motorboating	Speed skating
Barrel jumping	Autoracing	Dogsled racing
Karate	Judo	

Sports That Fit the Executive Woman's Image

Fly casting	Archery	Bobsledding
Tennis	Squash	Paddle tennis
Marathon running	Golf	Handball
Hunt riding	Polo	Skeet shooting
Harness racing	Sailing (competitive racing)	Fencing
Racquetball		

The woman executive does not even admit playing a sport unless she plays it well. She plays the way she works—competitively and to win. "You don't take your tennis racquet along unless you can beat the socks off most guys. There's no way a woman can afford to be the weak link in a tennis doubles match. And you don't even admit you own a set of gold clubs unless you can outgolf any guy you know," admonishes an executive. "Further, you never admit you play well. If you're terrific you say you play a little. Let the guys brag about your game. They will, don't worry. They'll also put you down if you don't play well enough to hold your own."

There is also a range of other activities—noncompetitive—that are acceptable to a woman's corporate image. Some of the executive's vacations may center around one or more of these activities.

• Downhill skiing	• Running	• Mountain climbing
• Trekking	• Scuba diving	• Sailing
• Soaring	• Horseback riding	• Rafting
• Cross-country skiing		

Her calisthenics, an activity essential to her routine fitness and well-being, are done in private. If junior members of her company attend a calisthenics class, she definitely avoids that class. It would be undignified to have her underlings watch her groan and pant. Her spare tire is her secret, just as much as her true hair color. She goes to classes where none of her colleagues will see her. If she's lucky, she has private calisthenics instruction. "I go by my calisthenics instructor's house on the way to work at 7:30 in the morning for thirty minutes every day," says one executive. "I have my workout guy come to my house four days a week," says another. "If he didn't come and push me I know I'd never do it. I'm just too burned out at night to motivate myself."

The recently popular exercise records and videotapes are perfect for the harried executive who does not want to spend the time to go to the gym or the money to hire an instructor. She puts the record or tape on her living room stereo at 7 A.M. and for twenty minutes kicks, pulls and stretches before she leaves for work.

If she has a cassette tape of her favorite exercise routine, she is able to keep in condition when she travels for business or goes away for the weekend. She takes a tiny cassette player with earphones, belts it around her body, and goes through her disco routine with no risk of disturbing anyone.

Moreover, the achieving woman has learned to play at least one game well to help pass the time on extended road trips with her colleagues. Ideally, she plays gin rummy or poker. These are two highly mobile games since they entail only a deck of cards. If she is new at these games, she has had secret professional instruction. She must be able to play tough and well as though she has played for years. She neither gloats nor sulks about the outcome—what is important is that she plays; winning and losing are incidental. She is perceived as a good sport—sportsmanship is elegant. It is important that she promptly pay any money wagered on a game.

She may play cards en route to corporate meetings on planes and in airports with her male associates. But she never sits in on late-night games—even when invited. She declines in the name of business. These are moments that are exclusively male, and she knows it. She knows there is nothing more out of place than a woman trying too hard to be one of the boys. She respects their time alone. She does not play touch football. She does not smoke cigars. She is not the only woman on the corporate baseball team.

The executive woman has learned how to play at least one gambling game, since her work takes her to Las Vegas for major professional meetings and to Monaco and the Bahamas for weekends between international business dealings. She can hold her own at one game, such as blackjack. She has more than adequately prepared by taking lessons from a pro—unbeknownst, of course, to her peers. If she plays either chess or backgammon well she finds a colleague who also plays. On extended trips she takes a small travel set along. She may play backgammon in casinos, too.

The woman executive has learned that trophies she gets from excelling at a game or sport look rather nice on her bookshelf as bookends. She does not frame citations and ribbons for her office. She knows that trophies make by far the strongest impression about her skill.

In summary, women who have made it to the top have recognized the extent to which sports and games have had an impact on the standard male-dominated corporate vocabulary and business framework. The successful woman compensates for any weakness in sports knowledge she may have inherited from her sociological background. Once again, she demonstrates how versatile she can be.

THE ART OF MAKING PRESENTATIONS

After a woman has buzz words and key financial concepts under her belt, she is ready to present her ideas and persuade her peers and boss to let her take on projects important to the future profitability of the company.

If the woman manager is ever going to influence the policy of her company, she has to be an effective communicator, in writing, in speaking one-to-one and in making group presentations.

"If someone can't write me an intelligent concise memo, there's no way I'm going to promote that person to any position of importance," avers a corporate chieftain.

The more eloquent a woman is, the better her chances. If she's got something smart to say and she expresses herself well she is already out in front of the pack.

She records herself on tape cassettes and rigorously critiques her voice to guarantee that it is firm, pleasant and well modulated. If she does not sound as she would ideally like, she works very hard to correct her problems, and may even (especially if her job requires numerous presentations) seek out a drama coach to help her develop perfect executive speech patterns. Moreover, she pays attention to regional speech patterns and adjusts her delivery accordingly. When she is making a speech in Texas she slows her pacing. When she is in New York she speeds up her delivery.

If her voice is fine but she has difficulty talking and gesturing effectively, she takes public-speaking courses. In these she can make her mistakes in front of other students—away from the boardroom.

When a woman is asked to make a presentation, she begins an intensive preparation. "Whatever you do, don't wing it," warns a woman whose success is the stuff that dreams are made of. "Practice, practice, practice." She uses graphics to spice up her presentations. Importantly, she orders her visual aids well in advance—so she can see them before her deadline. Then, if they are less than perfect, she can have them redrawn. The successful woman takes little for granted; she works on the assumption that what can go wrong, will.

Besides having excellent graphics, she spends several evenings organizing her speech. "I prepare exactly what I'm going to say and memorize all the major points I want to make. And I rehearse time and again to my dear patient husband. I do it over and over until it's second nature to me."

It requires rigorous practice and hours of work for an executive to appear to be completely at ease when she gives a twenty-minute presentation. A woman has to be prepared for a cold and foreboding boardroom or conference room with a big table, around which she will confront the basically inexpressive countenances of busy and demanding managers. She must not be flustered if someone gets up and leaves the room while she is addressing the group—other demands frequently neccessitate a phone call from an executive at a certain time. If one or two members of the group seated around the table leave during her presentation, the woman who is successful does not let the movement in the room disturb the pacing of her delivery.

The senior woman avoids at all costs any body language or gesture that makes her look nervous, shaky, aflutter or anxious. She appears calm, knowledgeable and confident. She adopts a demeanor that inspires confidence in those she addresses. She knows that since she is a woman she can do irreparable damage by fluffing her lines while she is the focus of male attention. She may refer to notes on an index card.

The canny manager is encyclopedic in her knowledge of her subject matter by the time she faces the committee members. But though she knows everything, she does *not* tell it all to the assembled group. She sticks to the high points and keeps her presentation as brief as possible.

"I hate to be told everything I never wanted to know. I want a succinct presentation," notes E. Camron Cooper. "If I want the details I ask for them after the initial speech has been given. I don't want someone to assume I want to go back and reinvent the wheel. But people get nervous and they try to impress you with how smart they are by telling you everything there is to know about a subject. That's a mistake. If they were smart they would know what is important and tell you only that. The other stuff they can keep as background in case senior management wants to question them."

The ambitious young woman also prepares for her presentation by studying as many different viewpoints as possible. She takes the other points of view and develops the objections that a certain perspective would raise to her own viewpoint. By the time she goes to the meeting she has developed strong answers to all the possible objections that can be raised. Once again, she may have notes or files with her to which she can refer for detailed information when a specific question is raised. She responds with thorough counterarguments that she has already carefully rehearsed. The more she is challenged, the better she looks.

Her cool, calm, intelligent presentation adds to her image as a competent, unflappable winner. If her performance is masterful, she is assured of being asked back time and time again. Each presentation she makes contributes to the credibility and visibility that are necessary to propel her to the top.

Conference Room No-No's

Stuttering
Forgetting a point
Jerky presentation
Shaking hands, trembling notes
Visual aids incorrect or out of sequence
Getting defensive
Voluntarily filling the committee in on too much of the background of a situation

Reading her presentation
Losing her place
Speaking too rapidly—a sign of nervousness
Addressing a committee "off the top of her head"
Taking objections personally
Adding cute and interesting asides

After she has impressed her senior management with her undeniable competence, the woman manager may be invited to sit in on key meetings in the conference room. She feels her role very gingerly. She looks carefully for signals as to what is expected of her.

When she is first invited to sit in on a meeting, the woman keeps a low profile. She listens and observes, noting not only the content of the discussions and the length of the average comment but what style of delivery seems to be most effective.

"It is perfectly okay for a woman not to say anything at all during a meeting, unless, of course, she is running it," observes Marian Sulzberger Heiskell, who spends much of her time in meetings. She is chairman of the Citizens Westway Park Advisory Committee, Council on the Environment of New York City and Gateway National Recreation Advisory Committee, and sits on several other boards. "Better to be quiet and not have everyone know I'm a fool than to speak up with something stupid so there's no doubt that I'm a fool," volunteers another woman whose days are often filled with meetings.

"I'm sure never to say something just to have said something," states a vice president in the media. "I particularly shy away from asking unimportant questions. Rather than being assertive, I prefer to be asked what I think. If I wait to be asked for my opinion, then when I give it it's more effective." She adds, "The important thing is not to try to impress someone."

Notwithstanding, prudent conference room conduct can prove very impressive for the ambitious woman. The conference room may be the first forum where top management can watch how circumspect and capable she is.

BLADDER POLITICS

The executive woman never excuses herself to "powder my nose." She excuses herself "to check with my office" or "wash my hands."

She tries not to go to the rest room unless there is a break and several men have first left to visit their toilet facilities. Since men often joke about the small size of women's bladders, the executive woman trys to avoid this stereotype by outlasting her male counterparts. If necessary, she drinks less liquid than the males she is involved with for day-long sessions.

She always avoids excusing herself at any time that entails men standing outside the door of her rest room to wait for her.

A convenient and unobtrusive time she can take a break is when she first enters a restaurant where the phones are adjacent to the ladies' room. She gives a colleague her beverage order and excuses herself to "make a call." She makes a call—and visits the rest room. This unobtrusive trip provides her with an opportunity to apply her lipstick carefully before lunch. Thus fortified, she avoids the need of reapplying it after the meal. Importantly, in the bustle of being seated and ordering her male companions are less aware of her absence.

When the meal is over, men usually wait to visit the rest rooms until they return to their offices. So does she.

The executive woman often is the only woman on outings with men. When she is on a long automobile trip and wants to stop, she merely uses the excuse of calling her office when she feels an urge to urinate. Thus, once again, she is mentioning her work and not her physical self as the reason.

When they all stop, she calls her office to check for messages—and then she stops by the rest room.

In summary, when the executive woman wants to visit a rest room for whatever reason, she always calls attention to her work. She never refers to her bodily habits, her gender, or any personal need.

6 MANAGING PEERS,

STAFF...

AND THE BOSS

The successful woman makes it to the top not only because she is good at her job but also because she is good at handling people. She makes full use of the "feminine intuition" women are reputed to have. She gets along well in a variety of different relationships. She is friend, colleague, boss and employee. She understands the differences in her various roles and behaves accordingly.

OTHER WOMEN

Most of the friendships of the accomplished working woman are with other successful women. "Friends I had before I became successful are not my friends anymore. Now there's nothing we have in common," notes a woman who has experienced meteoric success. She explains, "For one thing, I have a lot more money. Then too, they either don't understand what I've accomplished or they are overwhelmed by my achievements. The women I went to school with are no longer my equals."

Friendship involves communicating with each other about mutual experiences, so executive women keep female friends who have also triumphed in the work place. "My friends are attractive, powerful women. After all, birds of a feather flock together," allows an attractive, powerful woman. "My friends are all upper-level managers. They have to be to be comfortable with me and my success and my life-style," states another.

Finding time to develop new friends is difficult for the preeminent woman who is already juggling her office life and her private life.

One manager confides that she has been rebuffed in efforts to cultivate the friendship of other women in her own company. "Women are basically not supportive of other women in the same company. I sense that they talk to me more guardedly than men. My experience with women near my level has been that they are not open and warm to me."

Some women don't have any other women around with whom to establish any kind of relationship—positive or negative. "I've always worked in a male environment where I was the only woman. I have lots of men for friends in companies because there are not any other women at my level," notes a distinguished broadcast executive. "I've spent so much time dealing with men that I almost forget that women are out there too," says a president. She adds, "I don't think I'm a woman's woman. I get along best with men or couples."

THE FEMALE BOSS

Women give each other a bum rap, notes a banker. "I hear young women say they don't want to work with a woman boss. They enumerate any negative experiences they've had with women. Just as there are good male bosses and bad ones, there are good female bosses and bad ones. But the bad ones are the ones that make the big impression. It's important for women to learn to be supportive of other women and give them a break."

There seems no question that women are harder on each other than they are on men. They demand perfection of each other. Perhaps this is because each of them has had to overachieve to get ahead.

Also, it's possible that women are so tough on each other because they know each of them has to be perfect to make it possible for all of them to get ahead. When one woman fails it has a negative impact on other women in the company and future women who will be hired. She may herself never be given another chance. If a man fails, he suffers a setback but is usually given more opportunities to make good. Perhaps a corporate female manager does not formulate close friendships with women in her organization because of the possible taint if a woman known to be her close ally slips off the corporate ladder.

By the same token, a woman manager has to be very careful in promoting any woman who works for her. Should the junior woman blow a big deal, the executive's judgment will be called into question much more than if a junior male blew the deal. Although, if her male underling fails, she is more likely to be blamed than the man she oversees.

THE EXECUTIVE FRIEND

Although it is unusual for a woman executive to discover another high-ranked woman in her own company who is friendly, it sometimes happens. Because it occurs so rarely, it is only natural that the women circle each other warily, each wondering if the other is what she seems, each wondering if the other can be trusted.

Such a friendship between women proceeds slowly and carefully. It would be foolhardy for either woman to violate all the corporate rules she has learned to plunge impulsively into details about herself or her personal life. These friendships develop over a period of time while each gains the confidence of the other.

For one thing, women are very busy doing their jobs and juggling their lives. They may not take the time for idle chatter with another woman. Two such women, now closest friends whose careers have taken separate paths, occupied offices next to each other for two years before they paid attention to each other. "She was incredibly competent and professional but we always were both working like mad on separate projects that had nothing to do with each other," recalls one of the women. Their relationship began when they both coincidentally left their offices at 10 P.M. one evening. "We shared a cab home together. I said, 'I had no idea you worked these kind of hours too,' " relates the other. "We both shut our doors after hours and we each had no idea the other one was even there." The two women began occasionally sharing late cab rides home and ordering their office-delivered deli dinners jointly—although dinners were consumed separately behind closed doors since the women did not have time to talk. Within a year, trust had developed and the women began to be business allies. Even though they are now at different companies, they find each other's advice and counseling invaluable. Says one, "We have a rule. If one of us makes a mistake she tries to give the other one enough information so that she never slips into that particular pitfall." Both women are remarkably successful. Each credits the other for being an important sounding board and adviser. As one of them put it, "Our friendship is one of the most treasured aspects of my life."

Women know that if they lunch routinely with another woman, no matter what her expertise and professional skills, they run a danger of being dismissed at lunchtime by men as "going to lunch with the girls." So women who want to know each other better tend to develop their relationship after hours and on the weekend. They do not frequent each other's offices for the same reason they do not lunch together several times a week: They cannot run the risk of being perceived as clannish.

Women who become friends while working in the same company use the telephone for communication. They may speak to each other briefly on the phone every day once or twice. Nobody knows.

If an executive woman finds another high-ranked woman at her company whom she learns to trust as an ally and confidante, she is blessed. Once two women become close friends, they are able to drop much of the facade they may adapt for their corporate image. Illness, family and even clothes are topics they discuss openly in private.

One wonderful additional bonus in such a relationship is political. Having another woman as a solid ally in the same company provides an executive with a trusted conduit. Since the women are not seen together openly at the company, they may be privy to valuable information about each other that is spoken by others. Moreover, a woman friend who experiences the specific business environment of her company can provide an executive with a valuable, intuitively honed opinion on her management problems.

THE SUPPORTIVE SECRETARY

The other women easiest for top females to relate to in the corporate suite are often the secretaries. The executive woman finds for once that her gender is actually an advantage with executive secretaries of her male colleagues. "They tell me things about their bosses they'd never tell another man," boasts one. "If the upcoming meeting is going to dump some bad news on me that I don't know about, the secretary tells me, 'Maybe I'm talking out of school, but I think you should know that Joe is backing you up 100 percent but Bill is after your scalp,' " reveals an administrator. "It's wonderful to walk into a meeting and not be surprised when your parade gets rained on."

Yet another woman makes a conscious effort to cultivate secretaries. "I place my own calls. I use my first name. I say, 'Sarah, this is Sally. I know your boss is busy. But I only need ten seconds of his time when the meeting breaks up.' She is smart enough and aware enough to know it is important and that it will in fact only take ten seconds. Then she says to him, 'You've got tons of messages but first let me get Sally. She needs only a second. Speak to her while I get your next call. Adds the executive, "I always get my calls returned in record time."

Another says, "I'm the only woman on my floor who isn't a secretary. I think I'm their ideal. A couple of them are particularly marvelous to me. I always bring them perfume back when I visit Paris."

OPERATING IN A MAN'S WORLD

How well a woman is able to relate to her male peers is a function of how much support she receives from the top. If men on her level and above her perceive that the chairman of the company is solidly behind her, the going for a female executive is much easier. With pressure exerted from the top, men are forced to ostensibly acquiese to the presence of a female equal.

MALE COLLEAGUES

How well a woman fits into the male world is sometimes called the "comfort factor." This phrase refers to the extent to which a woman is able to put her male peers at ease. "If the chief executive officer is solidly behind a woman, it is remarkable how much more comfortable the men get. And how fast," notes one wag in mock surprise.

Even if men are ostensibly comfortable with her, a woman cannot help but be aware of a difference between the styles of the two sexes.

A woman simply cannot establish the same kind of rapport with men as men establish with each other. She probably is not invited to play golf with them on the weekends and she probably doesn't feel comfortable going to lunch with them as often as they lunch with each other. It is very difficult for her to gain access to the male corporate grapevine.

She is careful not to try to force her way into that community. That would cause the men to bolt the gates to their inner circle. It is far better for her to gently increase her access over a period of time. In the meantime, she performs at her job masterfully and continues to learn more rules and signals.

Since women are so conspicious and aware of being under greater scrutiny than their male counterparts, they have a keen awareness of how they are perceived. "The good news is that people around here say I'm organized and have my act together. The bad news is that some people assume I'm a bitch. There are those so prejudiced that they are even surprised when they find out I'm nice," confesses a sales executive.

"Behind my back they say I'm smart and I'm tough. They respect me. Everyone knows without a doubt that for me business is number one," says a financial chief.

THE FEMALE BOSS

The woman manager is aware that one of the handicaps of being a woman is that some people expect her to be a monster. "I know all about the stereotype of the bitch boss, the woman with concrete balls," remarks an industrial executive. "I bend over backward to undo that view of women. I make a great effort to develop people and make sure they advance."

The savvy female boss strives to run her department or division with an exceptionally fair hand. "It's better to create an atmosphere where both men and women are happy to work for you," notes one particularly supportive manager.

The executive woman knows it would be political suicide to obviously favor women in her department, to be the corporate "harem." The executive woman tries to have a balance between the number of men and women reporting to her. If she has a greater number of one gender, it is typically men. In some highly structured companies where there is pressure to promote people already in the company, enough women simply may not have been hired by the company for the executive to be able to find one qualified for her department.

PUTTING TOGETHER HER STAFF

When an efficient manager begins a search for a new staff member, she formulates a clear view of the type of personality and capabilities that will best suit the duties the position necessitates.

- She is careful not to hire an overqualified person who may be more personally appealing to her. That person will doubtless be bored and frustrated and will probably leave.
- She looks for a highly structured, not particularly imaginative, introverted person to keep tedious financial records.
- She looks for a cheerful extrovert with a high sense of personal structure for a tough sales position.
- She looks for a highly intuitive, carefully educated introvert to fill a sensitive research position.

One of the ways a manager shows her good judgment is in her ability to place the right person in the right job.

Once the executive formulates her image of the personal traits and skills to fit a position, she interviews all of the applicants within a few days. She asks questions that will reveal the characteristics she believes the job requires. She checks the "right" candidates' records carefully. She may personally call a current employer to check the reliability and competence of an applicant. If it is a top job she is filling, she may take the applicant and his or her spouse to dinner. The choice of a spouse reveals much about a candidate.

To reinforce her image as a decisive manager, the executive woman moves with all due haste to fill a position. Should she find that she has hired the wrong person, she does not hesitate to fire that person before serious damage is inflicted on the performance of her department. She tells her senior management the person misrepresented him or her self. If she uses an outside headhunter she has an advantage: She blames them, fires them and hires another firm. Ideally, she already has in mind an alternative candidate for the job, so she is able to move swiftly to replace the unsuccessful employee.

HOW SHE FIRES

When the executive fires an employee, she does so on a Friday or before a holiday weekend or planned vacation by the employee. This way the employee is able to clear out his or her desk during nonworking hours. The employee saves face and is also less likely to create disruptive ill will among the other staff members.

The successful woman tries to fire an employee without devastating the employee's ego. Usually she fires someone simply because the employee is in the wrong job or is unqualified to carry out the demands of the position. "There is nothing as miserable as being in the wrong position trying to do a job that does not suit your capabilities," sympathizes the executive. Perhaps she even suggests an alternative position in which she feels the employee will be more successful.

She never permits the employee's personal circumstances to deter her from severing the working relationship. If a prolonged illness in the family or a messy divorce is destroying the employee's performance, the successful business woman can be patient only to the point where her department's overall performance begins to be negatively impacted. After several warnings, she must let the employee go. Even with severe stress, a single employee cannot be permitted to make the entire department—and the executive woman—look incompetent.

GIVING AND TAKING CRITICISM

Moreover, the executive woman also is aware that the women who report to her may respond to criticism differently from men. The same tough stance she may routinely use on men who report to her may be softened for a woman. "Hey Dave, this is wrong. Fix it please, and soon," is softened to "Elena, I can't use this. It doesn't work. What I want is. . . ." The successful woman recognizes that the socialization process of the male culture includes blunt criticism and analysis, for instance, during team sport participation. On the other hand, women often are not prepared routinely to deal with brutal, blunt analysis.

By the same token, when a managing woman is herself harshly criticized, she steels herself against the blast. "I imagine that I'm on a football team and that I dropped the ball and the coach is furious," confides one successful woman. "I may have to give myself a little ego talk that night after I go home. But I also remind myself that tomorrow is a new ball game and that I am going to score a touchdown next time." She says she sometimes has to remind herself that the intensity of male criticism is not personal. It is all in the heat of the battle. The man who criticized her probably does not remember the intensity of his words. She tries to forget it too.

HER PERSONAL MANAGEMENT STYLE

The woman manager is more likely to maintain an "open" department. "I'm sympathetic about their problems," observes a banker. "I want them to feel free to come to me about anything. I want an atmosphere where they have a great deal of courage to be creative in their problem solving. I don't want fear to be the dominant motivator."

Although the mood may be relaxed, the executive does not confide completely in any one person who reports to her—or anyone else. "It's better not to say things off the record. It's better to be discreet," says a woman who works in the New York financial district.

She is not alone. The manager maintains an intentional distance from her employees. For instance, she never confides in matters of personality. "I rarely give an opinion about liking or disliking someone at the personal level.

And I use a general rule: If there is a question mark in your mind about whether to say something, don't say it. Further, it is not professional to ever talk about people when it's just a matter of curiosity," she warns.

Because of her care and tending of her staff, the overachieving woman enjoys a good reputation among junior employees as being someone who will promote them and teach them. "I've always been able to persuade someone to work for me," notes an industrial executive whose four top staff members happen to be all male. She adds, "I've been on the fast track. They know I'm going to move up and they hope they can move up behind me. I believe I'm highly regarded by other senior executives and have a reputation for being open and helping."

Notes another executive, "I'm not interested in whether my staff likes me or not. I want their respect. I also want them to feel they're getting something out of working for me. I always give my staff credit. Some people try to hog all the glory their staff generates. Not me, I give credit where credit is due. They appreciate that."

The successful woman manager treads a fine line between delegating responsibilities among her staff and delegating herself out of a job. The ideal solution is to divide the department responsibilities among three or four staff members. The executive gives each member clearly defined authority over a specific area. None of them overlap. Each staff member has his or her distinct arena and none of them is given an entire department overview.

Since she is the only one who holds all the cards in her department, the executive woman is careful to find a particularly capable and effective secretary. Moreover, a personal assistant may prove invaluable to the heavily burdened executive. The assistant is young, bright and ambitious, but not experienced enough to be threatening to the executive's job. The executive uses the young assistant's tireless energies to supplement her own. Both benefit, since the assistant gets a broad experience and contact base from being in the executive woman's world.

MOLDING HER OWN REPUTATION

The woman boss finds managing her own staff a satisfying part of her job. Since her own people are exposed to her skill on a daily basis, she finds it unnecessary to try to impress them. They naturally come to hold her in high esteem.

"Behind my back I am respected. They know I'm a hard worker. My employees might say I can be insensitive and demanding and blunt," ventures a banker. "But they will say I am an expert at politics. I know which strings to pull to get the job done."

"I try to find the middle ground between being too tough and too easy," comments a broadcast executive. "But I think they say behind my back, 'Don't fool with her.' "

A particularly distinguished manager is equally candid about what is said about her. "My employees say I have high expectations. Some say they are too high. Most say I am fair and that I have good judgment and a good sense of business. My detractors used to say I was a dragon lady," she smiles disarmingly. "Now they say I come on very strong."

MENTORS

Most of the current generation of executive women had to climb to the upper ranks the hard way, without any kind of a mentor, someone who regularly gave them assistance and guidance in shaping their career. "I invented myself out of thin air. I never thought about my career going anywhere. It simply happened," candidly confesses one successful woman. "I never had the luxury of any helping hand."

A mentor functions as a critical sounding board—an important service for the manager who is making critical decisions she has never faced before. A voice of experience can steer a young woman in the right direction. Sage advice from someone who has already been down a similar path can help her avoid multiple pitfalls. Making fewer mistakes, she progresses noticeably faster.

Frequently, the mentor is a senior executive at the same company as the achieving younger executive. However, she takes care not to be too closely identified with the man or woman who is giving her advice. "Don't get stuck with one person. Otherwise, when the conductor gets off the train, you have to get off too," warns an industrial executive. If a young executive is perceived as being sponsored by one senior person at the company, should that person retire or blunder and be forced out, the young woman can also be ostracized or relegated to an out-of-the-way position. The young executive tries to find multiple advisers in her company.

When she moves to a new company, the up-and-coming woman tries to find another set of mentors there to help, while continuing her previous contacts. "These men are my friends, my allies," states a communications executive. When one of her powerful mentors moved from one company to another, he called her up and offered her a better job at that company. Because of the men she picked to be her advisers—and who picked her—her career path is probably ten years ahead of where it would have been if she had tried to forge it on her own.

Obviously, the mentor a successful young woman chooses has to be smart and on the right track. Listening to bad advice can sabotage a great career. Selecting the right voice to listen to shows good judgment on the part of the junior executive.

The truly fortunate executive is the one who connected with a female mentor. Once again, the relationship has to involve mutual chemistry. "My role model sought me out. She said I reminded her of herself at my age, and she ended up having an important influence on the rest of my career. In almost every new situation I'd try to think how she would have done it. It always proved to be the right way," recalls one of America's elite women.

Sometimes a woman mentor can be remarkably influential in shaping a young woman's career. A brilliantly successful woman recalls that her mentor pursued her and hired her. "She was fifty and I was twenty-four. She made me a real assistant. I was an assistant on everything she was involved in. I went everywhere with her and met everyone she knew. Then she took a vacation and left me in charge for her. She went to the Yucatan, where she couldn't even be reached by phone. A crisis came up. I was able to handle it." When the mentor returned she promoted her assistant and launched her on a dizzily stellar career path.

Thus, a supportive mentor can provide opportunities that move a career ahead in giant steps. Moreover, the mentor is thrilled by the success of someone he or she advises.

A significant age difference between the mentor and the young career person is typical. Usually, today's executive woman chooses to be mentor to a man or woman who is at least half her age. The successful woman may act as a mentor to young assistants she brings into her organization. She uses their energies, ambitions and smarts to her great advantage and then fearlessly helps launch them into their own career orbits. The differences in their ages and experience mean that the younger employees, no matter how ambitious, are unlikely to pose any kind of threat to the job of the older, established executive. The executive continues to keep in touch for several years with the young people she has elected to mentor, acting as adviser, sounding board and intermediary in their behalf.

Although today's executive woman is likely to enter into a helping relationship with both young men and young women, she tends to spend more time with young women. "I know it's tougher being a woman—even today," comments one senior executive, who finds time late at night to return phone calls to a few special young women. "And it makes me so happy when I see talented young women get ahead. I help them because I know they need it more."

WHEN SHE'S READY TO MOVE UP

It is only when the executive woman has a definite promotion in mind that she begins to build a number two person who can assume her job when she moves up. This decision is made consciously at the advice of her senior management, who say, "Sure, we think you can handle a bigger job, but who will replace you?" "Give me three months and I'll tell you," is her reply.

The executive, who has long been aware of the limitations and capabilities of her senior staff members, usually has in mind two strong contenders for her job. Without informing those two of her specific intentions, she expands their responsibilities on specific projects to see which of them would best be able to handle her work load and continue to get along with the other senior staff members.

Good managers never turn the competition into an out-and-out confrontation. To do so means that the losing candidate will lose so much face he or she will elect to leave the company, leaving a large gap in the department. The most successful executive woman promotes the best-qualified person in such a way as to avoid creating irreparable damage to the good will in her department. When she moves up, the smooth functioning of her old department continues to enhance her reputation as an excellent manager.

When an executive resigns a position at one company to join another company, she is less concerned with leaving a smooth transition in her wake. She may surprise her management with her decision to leave and may merely suggest a particular staff member be considered to replace her. "I don't mind if they miss me when I leave," declares one woman. "It never hurts to be appreciated in your absence."

7 BUSINESS ENTERTAINING

The executive woman is in many social situations with her predominantly male peers. Although she might seem to be at a disadvantage, the dynamics of these occasions are largely within her control. It is, for instance, up to her to orchestrate the initial greeting of the social business encounter.

HER HANDSHAKE

Her greeting is firm, warm and predictable. Part of the grace of the executive woman is that she behaves with absolute consistency. She knows that people are more comfortable around her if they know exactly what to expect.

Her handshake sets the tone. As she greets visitors in her own office, she strides forward confidently with her right hand extended to clasp her colleague's hand in a warm, firm clasp. There is almost no such thing as shaking hands too often. When she goes to a reception she "works the room." She goes out of her way to shake hands. "Handshaking must have been invented by a clever male politician who was out of office," notes one irreverent wag. "Methinks it probably got him re-elected."

Moreover, the achieving woman has noticed how politicians and ministers make the people they come in contact with feel important by extending their right hand for the shake and then covering the clasped hand with their left. Known as the "minister's handshake" in some circles, this shake, when accompanied with a big smile and deliberate eye contact, is one of the favorite social greetings the executive woman employs.

When the encounter is a purely social setting and the colleague is held in particularly warm esteem, while she is firmly shaking the hand she reaches forward for a kiss in the air near the cheek or lightly on the cheek." This indicates in body language, "You are special."

HER FRIENDLINESS QUOTIENT

When the business occasion is supposedly "social," it is more informal. However, when the executive woman relaxes, she does not "open up." She is not lax or loose or free from responsibility and strict guidelines.

Entertaining business associates is really working—a fact the executive woman never forgets. She smiles more often, voices personal opinions on the weather, and makes small talk. She behaves more cordially. But the executive never "lets her hair down" when the social occasion is focused around business. She does not unbend. Her private life remains almost as closed when she is entertaining business associates as it is during business hours. Her private life is a world permanently closed to her work life.

THE HOME VERSUS THE RESTAURANT

In America, social business meetings often center around a mealtime. The executive arranges to have these business meetings at a restaurant.

Going to a restaurant offers several advantages. At a restaurant she can order what she wants to eat and drink without worrying about putting her hosts to extra trouble. The executive generally has dietary preferences, and she can indulge them at a restaurant without calling attention to them.

She avoids going to anyone's home for meals if at all possible. Few things are more socially miserable for an ambitious woman than accepting an invitation to the home of a prized client only to discover that the meal his wife has dutifully prepared is something the guest absolutely abhors, e.g. the executive detests lobster but finds it is the main entree. (The executive woman who wants to keep her client happy eats the lobster thermidor even though she detests it, and smiles the entire time.)

One executive suggests a compromise. "I prefer cocktails at business colleagues' houses," she says. "You can nibble at what pleases you and nobody notices."

The easiest way to divert a well-intentioned invitation from the home to a restaurant is to suggest a drink at the house with a meal at the restaurant. The successful woman uses this reasoning: "Why don't we go out to dinner and give your wife a night out on the town?" The wife is grateful and the executive woman has avoided being trapped in her dinner alternatives.

Moreover, a woman retains a greater degree of social control at a restaurant. As the hostess, she can ask for a menu ahead of time and set the pace of the meal. If the meal takes place at the executive's private club, she has great control over the tone and length of the meal—and over paying the tab. If she wants to be sure to be the one who foots the bill at a restaurant, she prearranges it with the restaurant management.

Importantly, at a restaurant dinner, no matter who is who's guest, she can more easily bring the meal to a close when she wants, without the other person being as aware of the fact that she may in fact be rushing the evening. If she is at the house of a business associate, her own good manners make her in essence a captive.

WHO PAYS?

The woman executive assumes she will or will not pay for the meal in accordance with the following unspoken American rules:

• If she is entertaining a client, she pays. Since her clients pay substantial fees for services such as advertising and products such as equipment, they generally expect to have their entertainment paid for by the supplier. Rarely will a male client challenge her paying the bill.

• If a woman initiates the meeting and it has nothing to do with a supplier-client relationship, she pays. The rule: The person who called and suggested having lunch asked the other person to lunch. The asker pays. This is where the problems arise. Some men still, even in today's tougher economic situation, suffer great discomfort when they witness a woman actually paying for their entertainment. The older the man, the more likely he is to balk at the woman's picking up the tab. The successful woman never makes a scene. She simply and graciously lets the insistent male pay. Usually, however, she structures the situation, e.g., goes to her private club, so that any awkwardness is obviated.

• If she frequently meets a colleague at a mealtime, they take turns picking up the tab.

THE BREAKFAST MEETING

This is one of the most controlled and businesslike of all mealtime meetings. At breakfast there is no liquor consumed and rigid time limits are completely acceptable. "Let's meet at 8 A.M. That gives me time to make a 9:30 meeting," she says. Thus the time frame is clearly established without any possible slight to her breakfast mate.

The place the executive selects for breakfast is always the one restaurant in town—every town has one—where the power brokers of the community gather for breakfast. Being amid a locally prominent crowd adds a certain palatability to the early hour of the meeting—an effective ploy if her counterpart is at all reluctant to meet early before business hours. Her breakfast date can then mention to someone, "The mayor is an early bird. I saw him at 8 A.M. breakfasting this morning at The Plaza."

If the woman meets at a restaurant where she regularly dines, she has a charge account with the establishment. That way there is no problem if she wants to pay the bill, because she quickly signs for it. If she is at a restaurant where she is not known and she wants to pick up the check but the business client is insistent about paying, she merely thanks him and permits him to pay. (When she dines with a woman, of course, the question of who pays is much less of an issue.) Breakfast is a relatively inexpensive meal in America, and no particular face is gained or lost by picking up the tab.

THE LUNCH MEETING

If a woman's responsibilities require that her lunch meeting be of a restricted length, she makes sure her lunch partner knows beforehand. "Lunch at 12:30? Let me check. We can do that if it is someplace nearby; I have a 2:00 meeting that day. Is that rushing it too much?" If the time would be too brief, she plans the meeting for another day or time. Knowing the length of the lunch gives both the lunch partners an opportunity to pace whatever business they want to cover. It also prevents either person from impulsively rushing away from the table before the other completes a slowly paced meal—both unexecutive and bad manners.

If the executive has initiated the lunch, she makes the reservations. She frequents a restaurant or lunch club where she has a charge account. There the bill is delivered to her for a quick signature. Thus she avoids any problem about her paying. The executive woman recognizes that since paying for a meal involves money, it involves power. It is more powerful to pay. She does not, however, make this fact a crusade. Business entertaining was invented for cementing alliances and creating new ones.

If she is lunching at a place where she has no charge account, with a male colleague who is outraged by the prospect of her paying, she never insists. She wants to achieve her business goal, not prove a point. She acquiesces with consummate grace—before hard feelings ensue. She recognizes that the fragile good will she creates during a single lunch can be undone by a tiff over who will pay. The obstinate sixty-year-old old-fashioned tycoon could leave wishing women would stay in their place.

If a man is always adamant about paying, she has her secretary note that fact—and arrange their future meetings only in her private clubs. (Actually, it is the act of paying that seems to make men uncomfortable when women pay the bill. If no money changes hands, and no credit card sits on the table, men seem more at ease. A quick signature by a woman seems to be quite acceptable.)

Under all circumstances, a woman selects a restaurant in keeping with her executive image. She rules out eateries with loud music or crowded tables. She chooses a place where she can count on an unhurried, cordial reception by the management and tables far enough apart to discuss serious business without fear of being overheard. She is conscious of prompt service, avoiding restaurants where the rhythm of the meal is interrupted by poor waiters.

Most importantly, the executive woman seeks out places that are frequented by the male power brokers and establishes a rapport with the maître d'. (This involves slipping him or her $5 to $20 on a regular basis.) She avoids places that are favorites of blue-haired matrons—such places dilute her image.

She is always the most up-to-date when it comes to knowing new hot spots that open in town. She gives both male and female meal companions lots of trendy names to drop. She knows that if she makes them look "with it" they'll be more accessible to her. They remember she makes them look good.

If the food at a restaurant is poor or if the service is dreadful, the successful woman ignores the fact. If her steak is not as she ordered it or her vegetables have been on the steam table for four hours, she says nothing. The successful woman never loses sight of the point of a business meal. Business meals are to favorably impress a client, ally or vendor. She wants the person she is meeting for lunch to recall that it was pleasant and that she is competent and resourceful. She does not want the client or colleague to remember that the food was bad, or that she made a scene.

DRINKS

Whether or not the executive orders a drink at lunch depends on with whom she is lunching. If she knows their habits and knows they do not drink alcohol, then she by all means declines alcohol out of politeness. If she is someplace with people she does not know, she merely asks them if they are going to have a drink. Her objective at a business lunch, after all, is to put her partners at ease and get the business done.

Regionally and nationally, lunch beverage habits vary. In the South of the United States, people often go to lunch at 11:30 A.M. and order coffee first before they order their lunch. In the Southwest, business people frequently meet at noon and order iced tea before they order their meal. In New York, business lunches begin at 12:30 to 1:15 P.M., and a glass of wine or a cocktail is typical before lunch is ordered. Coffee is served only with the last course.

The first-rate business woman takes her cues from the local inhabitants. It's very simple. All she has to do is look around to see what other people are doing.

Generally, if she orders a glass of wine, few people are offended. If for some reason she does not wish to drink it, she merely has one sip and forgets the rest. She decides how many glasses of wine she will consume at lunch according to the inclination of her guest. If it is a long lunch and the wineglasses are small as wineglasses go, and if her guest orders a second drink, she can comfortably order a second glass of wine. As a habit, however, she generally consumes no more than one glass of wine.

At lunch or dinner if everyone orders a cocktail before the meal and wine with the meal, the executive woman is free to do the same.

If she orders a cocktail, she is careful to avoid the traditional "old lady" drinks such as daiquiris, Tom Collinses, sweet vermouth and complicated rum drinks. She does not order drinks that come with little parasols in them. She does not order sweet sticky drinks, either before or after dinner. She orders what executive men order: scotch or bourbon, by brand name, on the rocks or with a small amount of water; a gin martini; or vodka on the rocks with a little club soda and a twist of lemon or, in summer, tonic water. After dinner, she orders a specific fine brandy. The executive does not mull over her drink order. She is definite about what she wants and specific about which brand and how it should be served.

If she is thirsty, she orders a bottle of mineral water in addition to her drink. She quenches her thirst with the water—never alcohol.

MEETING OVER COCKTAILS

If an executive hates to get up early in the morning and has little time for lunch meetings, her staple becomes the cocktail meeting.

Once again, she picks a place in keeping with her image: an elegant bar with good service and tables far enough apart to do business in private. Moreover, she looks for a place where the crowds are restrained and the clientele is elite.

She allows herself one mixed cocktail drink or two small glasses of wine for an hour-and-a-half cocktail meeting.

She can contain the length of this meeting by stating simply that she has a business dinner she has to leave for at a given hour. She says this even if she wants to cut the meeting short for personal reasons. It is much more businesslike to excuse herself for business reasons than say, "I told my husband I'd stop by the deli on the way home and that I wouldn't keep him waiting beyond 7:30 for dinner." The executive woman does not want to be viewed by her business associates as just another harried, overworked wife and mother.

As at breakfast or lunch, if she requested the cocktail meeting, she asks for the tab. If the male insists, she lets him pay. "Men seem the most adamant about paying for drinks. Lord knows why!" confides one executive. She notes that a cocktail bill is usually not substantial. "If he insists on paying, I say thank you very much and smile," she continues.

COCKTAIL PARTIES

The successful woman knows that at cocktail parties what is important is that she meet, greet and be seen. She doesn't have to stay very long to accomplish this. If she arrives at the first moment the invitation indicates, ahead of the rush, she is highly visible. She explains to her host that she has a dinner meeting and leaves.

If she's the first one to come to a cocktail party and she leaves in thirty minutes, she's more visible than if she arrives in the middle with the crush of people and stays for two hours. The reason is simple: The more people there are jammed into a room the harder it is to be seen.

DINNER ENTERTAINING

The woman executive who wants to save some of her time for her private life limits her dinner functions. "I consider dinner meetings among my working hours," states a division president. "Since my work day begins at 7:30 in the morning, a two-hour dinner beginning at 7:30 at night means a fourteen-hour day. That's the pits!" she exclaims.

EVENING WEAR

At dinner meetings, the executive woman often wears her regular business clothes, dressed up perhaps, e.g., diamond earrings and a diamond pin or brooch with one or two elegant diamond highlights. "I prefer my work clothes for business dinner," notes a Wall Street executive. "I want them not to forget I'm a business woman. I let the executive wives do all the glory dressing."

If an executive does choose to change and the city is a dressy one, she may change to a dark velvet suit with a satin blouse, or a simply cut long-sleeved, high-necked dress. "When I dress for dinner I always keep in mind the difference between the way Mrs. Reagan, the First Lady, would dress compared to Mrs. Thatcher, Britain's prime minister. Mrs. Reagan is the quintessential corporate wife, as it were, and Mrs. Thatcher is the quintessential executive. While one might wear a red off-the-shoulder stunning dress, the other would wear something simple and elegant you would not remember. Mrs. Thatcher does not want to be remembered for what she wears. When you look at her you think how successful and powerful she is. I keep Mrs. Thatcher in mind when I dress for a dinner party," says coal consortium chairman of the board Mary Eileen O'Keefe, a particularly elegantly attired executive.

THE QUICK GOODBYE

One executive woman has learned a ploy that enables her to duck out from some of the impersonal association dinners with a cast of thousands that she is required to attend. She admits, "I figure that after you are seated you only see the people seated with you. The bulk of the socializing is done before dinner at the cocktail party. I go to the cocktail party early, greet everyone I know, and accomplish the contacts I want to make." During the rush to be seated for dinner, she leaves. The best news: No one notices! "Sure, I have already paid for dinner at these kind of deals," she remarks. "But I would have happily paid twice as much not to go. The food at big dinners is always rotten anyway."

When she is out of town and has a severely constrained time frame and many people she wants to see, she will have dinner meetings every night. "I don't mind those dinners when I'm on the road," says another executive. "I don't have a private life when I'm traveling anyway."

If her hosts prefer to have her join them at a club, the executive is careful to arrange for her own transportation. She knows too well how people with a less constrained time frame dally over drinks after dinner, extending the engagement until the wee small hours. To avoid getting caught in this trap, if she has no car of her own she either rents one or arranges for the hotel to have a car pick her up at a prearranged time. Thus, at 9:30 or 10 P.M., when the maître'd whispers that her car is waiting, it gives her an opportunity to bring at least her part of the evening to a close.

The executive must learn how to extract herself from dinner company without hurting their feelings. One of the pitfalls of being so successful, so charming and so adept at small talk and business is that the company of the achieving woman is in demand. Business people enjoy doing business with her, but sometimes it's overwhelmingly time-consuming. "I have to prepare for an early-morning meeting" usually gets her out of any place. Once again, she focuses on business. Preparing for a meeting is a more effective excuse than a personal statement such as "I'm bone weary and need to sleep."

DRINKS

Whether a woman has a drink and if so what she drinks is determined by several factors beyond her personal whim.

The location is one factor. Some parts of the United States and other parts of the world frown on women drinking. The successful woman has her staff do her homework for her in advance so that she knows about any local constraints.

If the others present at the meeting are drinking only wine, the woman drinks wine also. Under no circumstances does she order a double scotch on the rocks. If she does not like wine, she accepts one glass and takes tiny sips. If everyone else orders a cocktail, the ambitious woman orders one also, whether she wants it or not. As a woman she is too conspicious to risk being perceived as a prude, teetotaler or possible reformed alcoholic. She raises her glass to her lips for any toasts. If she really does not want to drink her drink or is in fact a teetotaler, she simply does not drink it, or she looks for a plant or another glass to empty it into.

The executive woman never drinks to excess and never stays out late "drinking with the boys." Such conduct is simply beyond the pale. She has become successful and accepted on her own terms without resorting to drunken camaraderie. Any high-spirited, champagne-filled evenings she has are entirely separate from her business life. "Serious partying" is shared with friends—not colleagues.

MEETING OVER NIGHTCAPS

The executive is aware that an invitation to have a drink after dinner can be construed as a sexual encounter if not handled very carefully. She avoids such meetings whenever possible. "On a scale of one to ten, if ten is the highest rating for a time to transact business, nightcaps rate a zero," snaps one executive.

However, there are rare occasions when nightcaps are inescapable.

The reasons for accepting such an invitation or initiating one must be clear-cut.

• She or the other executive have been tied up in meetings all day, have not had a single moment to meet, and must get together before the following morning.

• Both have been in meetings together all day and, as close allies, want to compare notes.

• One of them is on a whirlwind visit into the other's town and they simply want to greet each other in person.

Even if the business at hand is very serious and the circumstances are crystal clear, the executive is very careful to restrict her drinking. She also keeps the meeting brief: Half an hour is enough.

She is firm about terminating this meeting. Once again, she uses the grounds that she has more work to do that evening and an early appointment in the morning. Under no circumstances does she imbibe too much or remain with her companion long enough to see him or her overindulge. She learned long ago that one of the best ways to avoid embarrassing situations is to leave before they develop.

BUSINESS DINNERS WHERE SPOUSES ARE INCLUDED

Generally, unless her marriage is imminent and her fiancé accompanies her the unmarried executive attends large business dinners alone.

She dresses simply. If the dinner is black tie, she wears a long dark dress. She opts for a high-necked, long-sleeved, simply cut "background" dress. She avoids anything deliberately sexy: Slit skirts and cleavage are for the executive wives. As usual, she resorts to important jewelry for adornment—or wears none. If the dinner is informal, she dresses as she would for any dinner.

If she is unmarried, her social road with the wives of her male colleagues can be more difficult. "It's the one time I break the rule about personal privacy," confides one particularly young and attractive executive, "I manage to mention to the wives at some point in the evening that I am very committed to a man in my life. If I didn't in fact have one, I'd invent one."

The wives of the men she deals with are a primary motivator in the executive woman's decision to invite an escort. "If it's a small dinner, I find it's often more relaxed if I bring a male escort. That way he can fetch my drinks, permitting less interaction between me and my host. This is a big help if my host's wife is the jealous type. Besides, taking a date provides an even number for sit-down dinners," observes an unmarried executive.

While a professional woman may take pains to put to rest any fears a male colleague's wife may have about her intentions, she can do only so much. "I knock myself out to show it's his work that I'm impressed with," says another executive. "If his wife is jealous, there isn't very much I can do. Being jealous is a problem she has independent of anything I've ever done." Agrees another: "The wives who are secure and achieve on their own and have good self-images are not threatened."

"If I need to discuss business with a male colleague at a cocktail party, for instance, I always ask his wife where he is and say I need to talk to him about a pressing business issue," relates a broadcast executive. "Five hundred people in the room, but his wife always knows where he is. She gets him and brings him to me. Then when she sees us talking intently she knows we're talking about business."

"I try to avoid talking about business over dinner so that a man's wife doesn't feel left out," says an attractive young banker. "Sometimes men's wives have read about me in a magazine and they are already scared of me when they first meet me."

If she is married and has her own husband along, she has an easier row to hoe, especially if he is successful in his own right. He is known to her colleagues because of his own success in the business or professional community, and is welcomed by her male peers with esteem and cordiality. Also, merely be being present, he allays the suspicions of the insecure corporate wife who imagines every unmarried woman in the office is out to seduce her husband.

GETTING TO KNOW THE CORPORATE WIVES

Almost all male executives have children. Once a woman executive has both a husband and children, it is easier for a corporate wife and mother to relate to her. Children can play an important role in helping an executive establish relationships with these women.

Notes an executive mother, "The baby proved to be a great icebreaker. Before, the wives had their home life and I had my work life and there wasn't much that we had to discuss. Now that I have a child there is a big difference in the way women react."

Just having children, even if the marriage has been dissolved, may be enough to facilitate comfortable relationships with other executives' wives; Notes an unmarried division president who has two young children, "The children give us shared interests. I talk about domestic matters at length with them. I like a lot of the wives and we're friendly in a nice chatty gossipy hausfrau kind of way. Besides, our children go to school together."

The executive woman recognizes that the better known she is to the wives of her peers, the less likely she is to be feared as a possible husband-napper. She goes out of her way to talk with the wives. "I let the wife set the tone about what she wants to talk about and then that's what we pursue," says one executive woman.

"When wives are present I never touch a man—not even on the arm. Shaking hands is the extent of our physical contact. I don't give wives any fodder to feed their insecurities," avers another high-powered woman.

An investment banker has discovered that there are political advantages in trying to cultivate the executive wife. "Once you develop a rapport with the client's wife, she is on your team. In the long term that is a factor in my favor. If she mentions me to her husband in a favorable way maybe I'll get more business from him."

The president of a food franchise chain agrees. "I don't wear jewelry when I am around my clients' wives. When I entertain them I dismiss my household staff (a maid and a butler) and cook and serve myself. I don't want them to be intimidated or jealous. I want them to like me. I present myself so that they don't perceive me as being as successful as I am. I talk about my husband and housekeeping and my children. I try to make them forget I'm even a business woman."

"The more senior I get, the more interesting the men's wives are," says Dr. Dorothy Gregg. "The wives of executives are interesting. They're often involved in the pulse beat of the cultural and rehabilitative community projects. They're doers, too. I always learn from them."

Notes a senior industrial executive, "Wives of executives are expected to play a leadership role in strategic cultural activities. I find out what each woman's activity is. It is of critical importance to find what their focus is, talk to them about it and treat them as the equals they usually are."

MANAGEMENT MEETINGS AT RESORTS

If a meeting includes opportunities for swimming and sunbathing, the executive woman exposes herself only with discretion. Under no circumstances does she wear a bikini. A one-piece maillot is for her. She is careful to cover up in a head-to-toe wrap whenever she is around her colleagues or their spouses. Whether her body is beautiful and perfect or marred and flabby she does not want her body to become an issue. Wisely, she keeps it concealed. "Don't flaunt it if you've got it and don't flaunt it if you don't have it," declares a high-ranked woman.

At night, when many women at resorts wear backless dresses and slit skirts and show themselves off in sultry resort sexiness, the executive remains as simply dressed in linens with crisp antique laces as she does in the office. Her style never changes. The sexiest dress she would consider wearing? A sleeveless red one!

"The worse thing I can imagine is having the chairman of the board of my company see me in a provocative dress and exclaiming, "Migod, Sarah, I never noticed you have such a great figure," notes one executive. "My resort wear looks like converted office wear. My idea of jazzy is a simple linen dress."

THE ESCORT

If a meeting entails overnight accommodations, the unmarried female executive does not share a room with her man even if she is engaged to be married or living with him (for years!). If she is known to be deeply involved or feels that an escort's value as a social buffer outweighs any "tsk-tsk's" that may be uttered by her colleagues' older wives, she invites a man but puts him up in a separate room. His room does not adjoin hers.

Bringing along a different man each year can undermine an executive's effectiveness. "Nobody can put up with her," her peers will say. "Maybe her roving eye will alight on my husband," an insecure wife will think.

THE SPOUSE SCHEDULE

If a meeting lasts for several days, an executive woman's husband is in a strange quandary. Since spouses have traditionally been housewives, agendas for spouses are planned around visits to women's shops and traditional women-oriented events.

Just as the wife who is working outside of the home has difficulty attending daytime spouse events while her husband is involved in business meetings, the executive woman's husband has work of his own that often interferes. Usually, it is sufficient for executive husbands to attend only the one most important dinner meeting and cocktail party.

"My husband hates being the only male spouse," confides one executive. "He copes with it but he hates it. Of course he comes when I ask him, but I only ask him if it's really important." He tries to arrange his schedule to be present at the single most important dinner at her company's annual managers' meeting. He spends that night and takes the first flight out the next day.

CHOOSING AN ESCORT

If the executive woman has no man in her life whom she is interested in marrying, she chooses a special kind of man to help her out with her business entertaining. She brings an unmarried male who not only, of course, has social graces but is known and highly regarded by all of her colleagues. He is from a business, or in a career that is in no way competitive to hers. Thus, if she is in publishing, he works on Wall Street. If she works in finance, he may have a nonbusiness position, such as chief government economist or noted professor.

Thus, she used her unmarried status to her advantage: She picks a social mate *not* for the reasons she would necessarily use to choose a husband. She picks one who is eminent, witty, reliable and urbane.

DATES AND ESCORTS FOR THE SUCCESSFUL WOMAN

If an executive's colleagues admire the man she has with her, they automatically elevate their assessment of her. Her sexuality and femininity are automatically reinforced in their eyes without her having done anything except exercise good judgment. Her date is not only attractive physically but successful in areas that are instantly recognizable to the men she deals with. "That Judy is one tough cookie, but she must have something going for her I don't know about," runs the private conversation of her male colleagues. "Do you know who she dates? Ted Golden, the famous golden boy of tennis! Neat guy!" Or, they think to themselves, "Judy had the district attorney as her date. No wonder she knows the inside track." Judy has enhanced her image merely by the man she associates with. That is the easiest step ahead she can make—enhancement by association.

If a woman manager has discovered that the sexiest men in her life are absolutely unacceptable to her male colleagues, she simply keeps her real sex life a secret.

If carpenters and golden beach boys turn her on, she keeps it a closely held secret. She pursues her penchants in out-of-the-way places where she is most unlikely to be seen by any of her peers. A San Francisco banker is quite safe fraternizing with beach boys in hippy-strewn Venice in Southern California. No one she works with would dream she wears cutoffs and T-shirts. If they saw her they wouldn't recognize her.

Moreover, the executive woman has learned that in pursuing nonexecutive men, her own success may be a detriment. It may frighten a man off. To avoid this problem, she simply tones down what she really does, how much she makes or has achieved. She knows the truth would threaten him. So she does what men do so well: She is less than candid.

If she does not want Jake, who is wonderful and sexy and totally nonexecutive, to ever call her at the office, she explains that she has a mean boss who would fire her if she were to receive a personal call. Chances are Jake can relate to that. If Jake sees through the ruse, she may choose to drop him.

The unmarried woman manager also keeps any male homosexual friends in the closet. She understands that the male corporate scene is rigidly macho and ill at ease with alternate life-styles. If she is seen in the company of gay men, she is immediately the victim of innuendo and gossip, mostly behind her back where she can ill defend herself. "Did you see? She is such a ball breaker she can't even get a real man," is the first report that the male corporate community will quickly circulate after she shows up with a gay man at a business function.

The only exception to the rule barring gay men as escorts is in the fashion and design fields, where some gay men have become household words, extremely successful designers and merchandisers. Since money talks, these men have earned respect in their industries based on their ability to generate sales. Their financial success offsets their perceived sexual liabilities.

If she is gay herself she certainly does not advertise the issue since many corporate men are even more threatened by a gay woman than an obviously gay man. Just as gay men in the traditional corporate world frequently bring a woman escort to functions where spouses are included, a homosexual woman shows up with an acceptable male escort in tow. The successful woman knows that by maintaining an appearance of conventional sexuality she is free to pursue what ever sex life she likes—in private.

ACCEPTABLE DATES
(Men her peers will immediately respond positively to)

Occupation	Reason for Positive Male Response
SENIOR PARTNERS OF MANAGEMENT CONSULTING FIRMS, ACCOUNTING FIRMS AND LEGAL FIRMS. Their names are part of the firm's name	Powerful and instantly recognizable as "old boys"
EMINENT PROFESSORS. Experts on subjects related to her corporation and known by reputation to her male colleagues	Authority and a different perspective
PHYSICIANS. Internists, cardiologists, all kinds of surgeons, eye, ear and throat specialists	They make lots of money. They bring a different perspective.
PLASTIC SURGEONS. If she is above suspicion of having availed herself of their services	Glamorous profession
MAJOR SPORTS FIGURES. 1st tier—Major league football stars, Champion golfers, Top 10 tennis players, Car racing champions	Her peers will be incredibly impressed. They will ask for autographs. Her reputation soars.
2nd tier—Major league baseball stars, Major league hockey stars, Major league basketball stars	These men are less likely to be household words. The remarkable size of a tall basketball player might detract.
TELEVISION AND MOVIE PRODUCERS	Connote glamour, power, money
NEWSPAPER PUBLISHERS	Glamour, Power
MAJOR NEWS BROADCAST PERSONALITIES	Glamour, Power
MAJOR TV OR FILM STARS	Glamour

ACCEPTABLE DATES
(Men her peers will immediately respond positively to)

Occupation	Reason for Positive Male Response
HIGHLY VISIBLE ELECTED OFFI-CIALS	Power
OWNERS OF LOCAL SUCCESSFUL AND WELL-REPUTED BUSINESSES	Money
THE CHIEF OF POLICE	Power, Clout
REAL ESTATE DEVELOPERS	Money, Power, Clout
INVESTMENT BANKERS AND MONEY MANAGERS WHO MAN-AGE MILLIONS OF DOLLARS	Power
PROFESSIONAL BIG GAME HUNTERS	Glamour, Romance, Excitement
IMPORTANT ARCHITECTS	Prestige. Businessmen can relate to buildings.
SUCCESSFUL MEN TEN YEARS HER JUNIOR	She must have something if she attracts handsome winners who "could have anybody."

UNACCEPTABLE DATES
(Men a woman takes home, but not to meet the president)

Occupation	Reason for Positive Male Response
STUDENTS	The exception would be someone doing a fascinating study under prestigious auspices.
PROCTOLOGISTS AND URINARY SPECIALISTS	When they say what their occupation is, what do a woman's colleagues respond with? Conversation dies.
GYNECOLOGISTS	Same as above.
JUNIOR PARTNERS	Not impressive enough unless a member of an important family.
ASSISTANT PROFESSORS	The exception would be the obviously brilliant writer of an industry-rocking study.
ACTORS WHO ARE NOT CURRENTLY WORKING	Unless they are famous.
MODELS	Viewed suspiciously by businessmen.
DECORATORS	Businessmen are not interested in men who do "women's work."
ROCK BAND PERFORMERS	Men over 40 are pre-Beatles in experience. A famous old crooner would be acceptable.
BOXERS, WRESTLERS	These are not as upscale as members of team sports.
REAL ESTATE SALESMEN	It is difficult for them to quickly telegraph their excellence to her peers.
ALL SALESMEN WHO ARE NOT VICE PRESIDENTS	Their business cards won't impress a woman's colleagues.

UNACCEPTABLE DATES
(Men a woman takes home, but not to meet the president)

Occupation	Reason for Positive Male Response
OPERA SINGERS	The exception would be Pavarotti—who is married.
LOCAL ARTISTS	Businessmen often do not have (1) knowledge or interest in art or (2) respect for men who opt out of their chosen corporate environment.
SHOP MANAGERS	Their responsibilities will not impress a woman's upwardly mobile peers.
POLICEMEN, FIREMEN	They don't have the kind of clout ambitious men want to cultivate.
PLANT MANAGERS	Unless the plant is huge and they are vice presidents with a major company.
LOW-TIER SERVICE PERSONNEL: ELECTRICIANS, CARPENTERS, REPAIRMEN, INSTALLERS, CONSTRUCTION WORKERS, BARTENDERS, WAITERS	Businessmen want to meet people they cannot hire for small amounts of money. High-priced consultants would be fine.
NEWSPAPER REPORTERS	These inhibit conversation. Many businessmen feel both overly self-important and paranoid.
SKI INSTRUCTORS, LIFEGUARDS	Champion skiers might be okay. Otherwise, businessmen are both jealous of their physiques and disdainful that they opted out of the corporate arena.
CHIEF COMPETITORS OF HER COMPANY	Her colleagues will rumor "pillow talk" is damaging the company.

UNACCEPTABLE DATES
(Men a woman takes home, but not to meet the president)

Occupation	Reason for Positive Male Response
MAJOR SUPPLIERS TO HER COMPANY	Her colleagues will suspect a "sweetheart deal."
VERY OLD MEN, UNLESS THEIR WEALTH IS LEGENDARY	Her colleagues will say she can't find a "real" man. Money and power, of course, make them quite acceptable.

THINGS AN EXECUTIVE WOMAN NEVER DOES FOR BUSINESS ENTERTAINMENT

- Closes down the bar and discos the night away with a sloshed male colleague.
- Reveals at last what a sexy lady she is—showing up at a corporate dinner party with deep cleavage and a slinky slit skirt.
- Proves she can outshine all the other women present—all of them married to her colleagues.
- Brags to a male colleague's wife about how much fun he is.
- Insists on paying the bill—just to prove a point about women's lib.
- Shows that she can hold her liquor better than any of the guys.
- Sits in a hottub with the guys.
- Brings a gay escort to a business function unless he's a household name.
- Brings her female lover out of the closet.

8 MANAGING
TRAVEL

The executive woman has an unflappable and distinctive elegance that wins the admiration of anyone who has ever seen her travel. She has not in fact been everywhere on the planet, but she has an arsenal of travel information and style that puts her as much at ease in Hong Kong as in Hamburg or Houston.

This is no accident. The executive woman always has a definite, well-thought-out plan. Simply, she does her homework before she leaves.

HOMEWORK

The executive woman has researched the climate and possible temperature extremes in cities where she is destined. She knows in advance whether to expect snow, wind or monsoon. She knows if there are likely to be travel problems and she has anticipated these factors in her dress, schedule and commitments. She knows the cities that have the most unpredictable weather and packs a winter coat and a summer suit for the same city just in case.

Moreover, the executive woman is prepared for the currency of any place she lands. She has $50 in small bills in foreign currency to pay for taxis and food in the airport of any country she lands in. She knows that foreign exchange offices frequently are closed even in major airports.

She carries foreign currency even if she has no intention of spending time in a particular country. The vagaries of air travel are such that a scheduled two-hour layover can last two days.

The executive woman also has a good supply of $1 bills in U.S. dollars, knowing that as a last resort American dollars can get things done.

Further, the executive woman is aware of the national holidays and customs of the countries she visits. She is aware of the feelings of native men toward business women and knows whether or not she is at a disadvantage because she is a woman. If in doubt, she should assume she is.

Moreover, she has a basic phrase book on the country's language, and prior to arriving has learned how to say "hello" and "thank you" and "Do you speak English?"

LUGGAGE IS NEVER CHECKED

Whether she is traveling to Alaska for two weeks or Washington, D.C. for three days, the executive woman never carries more than two pieces of luggage and a briefcase. "I carry my luggage because the men do. When we arrive at our destination they don't want to stand around and wait for me," notes Elaine Linker.

The successful woman carries one piece of luggage that is the regulation size to fit under her seat and one piece that is for hanging clothes. To give herself flexibility, she has both shoulder straps and regular handles on her luggage *and* her briefcase. If necessary, all three items can be carried on her shoulders and her hands left free. In a driving rain when she is holding an umbrella and fumbling for the door of her rental car, those three shoulder straps are indispensable. Her hands are also free to hand open her passport at customs and to fill out visa forms. A suitcase on wheels leaves the traveling woman similar freedom.

These two pieces of luggage are permitted as carry-on luggage on most commercial airlines around the world. The successful woman has her travel agent select a larger aircraft, when there is an option, so that she may carry her luggage into the cabin with her. Some regional "commuter" airlines lack enough space to accommodate her bags. She avoids traveling on these when possible.

There are several advantages to carrying her luggage on board. For one thing, the luggage is not at the mercy of airline personnel so it never gets waylaid or lost. Also, since it is in her hand, the luggage makes tight schedule connections that luggage in the luggage compartment cannot possibly make. "I learned to carry my own luggage the hard way," confesses a corporate chieftain. "My luggage missed the connection when I arrived one morning in Oregon. I had to go straight to a press conference I was giving. There I was on television in clothes, face and hair left over from the previous day. My luggage arrived that afternoon. I was already on my way home."

Moreover, having her luggage in hand gives a woman added flexibility about changing her plans quickly. Flexibility is something the executive woman values. Her time is precious and being flexible can save time.

Further, if she personally carries on her luggage there is less possibility of its being crushed or broken and its contents ruined. Hang-up clothes bags travel hung up in the aircraft. In this way they arrive much less wrinkled and crushed. "I carry one wrinkle-proof outfit when I go to Europe," says New York–based American Express executive Sandra Meyer. "I arrive in London at 7 A.M. London time and check into my hotel. I change into the wrinkle-proof outfit. I send my travel clothes to the one-day cleaning service and everything that is wrinkled goes to be pressed. When I return from my meetings at the end of the day everything is fresh in my closet."

The executive woman plans ahead and anticipates the worst. She knows that if something goes awry and she has no contingency plan, she is more likely to lose face in the male community than a man in similar difficulties.

PACKING FOR OVERNIGHT TO THREE DAYS

The executive always takes another suit along—just in case a disaster befalls the clothes she is wearing. It is always possible some steward will pour orange juice in her lap on the plane. On short trips, she indulges in the luxury of taking another color from the color of clothes she wears on the plane, e.g., she takes a gray suit and shoes and wears a brown suit and shoes. "Luxury is a change of shoes," notes a woman who travels about one-third of the time for her multinational company.

To maximize her options, she takes plain blouses that can be worn with either suit. If she is planning fancy dinner meetings, instead of packing a change of clothes she packs a change of jewelry. For evening, she merely tucks a pair of diamond earrings and another strand of pearls in her briefcase pocket. "I pack a black skirt and blouse which I wear in the daytime with a coordinated plaid jacket," says a top executive. "At night I merely wear the skirt and blouse without the jacket. With pearls and a brooch it gets me through dinner anywhere."

The executive woman also takes the following items regardless of where she is going or for how long:

• Driver's license and possibly passport.
• Variety of credit cards.
• Membership cards to VIP lounges in airports.
• Cash in small bills and two $100 bills.
• A detailed itinerary for her reference with telephone numbers of every place she is going and everyone she is slated to see—her secretary has a copy. So does her spouse.
• Magnifying makeup mirror.
• Collapsible umbrella—easily accessible.
• Rain hat.
• Makeup kit—including nail polish and emery board.
• Toiletry kit including sanitary napkins, tampons, and any habitual medication.
• Spare stockings.

PACKING FOR LONG TRIPS OR TRIPS TO SEVERAL CITIES

The executive woman still takes only two pieces of luggage, albeit the luggage may be more fully packed.

The longer the trip, the more carefully she pulls together different suits and blouses, using the same color scheme, thus limiting the shoes and accessories. Trips to multiple cities are easier than an extended visit to one town in the sense that she can wear the same outfit time and time again without that fact being noticed by the people she is meeting, because she sees new people in each new city. "I have to check my luggage when I go to Paris," says a fashion executive. "Unfortunately, I'm with the same people day in and day out for a week and I don't want to wear the same outfit twice." She plans each day's and each night's outfit for her stay.

If she has a black-tie dinner to attend, she may carry along one long skirt that matches one of her regular suit jackets, thus avoiding the necessity of another dress. The ultimate in flexibility is a long ultrasuede skirt that matches the jacket of a daytime ultrasuede suit. It is appropriate in every climate of the globe except an extremely tropical one. "Life without ultrasuede would be a lot more difficult," notes a financial executive who says she "lives in it on the road."

If she is traveling rapidly from city to city, the executive takes a couple of drip-dry blouses made of a fabric that looks exactly like silk, in case she stays at a provincial hotel where there is no one-day laundry service. She also carries a small travel iron so that no one suspects she is wearing a drip-dry creation, or that she washed it out herself and pressed it the night before. Washing and ironing are not part of her executive image.

The executive woman never needs to worry about whether she is appropriately dressed for any particular culture, because her standard business apparel is absolutely acceptable all over the globe. She is considered perfectly dressed everywhere except a few Middle Eastern countries. That's hardly a problem: The men of those few backward countries would refuse to do business with her anyway. She wouldn't be likely to blunder into such a situation. Her research on the subject would have had her fully prepared.

TYPE OF LUGGAGE

The executive woman knows that beautiful leather luggage is heavy to carry and impresses the bellmen at hotels more than it impresses her peers. She also knows that when she is racing to catch a plane, weight becomes paramount to her. So she buys simple pieces of nylon luggage as lightweight as possible. She has two different sizes of hang-up luggage and under-the-seat bags. The smaller ones make the short, simple trips with her.

Since she carries her luggage with her so much, she picks it in a color that coordinates with the color she is most likely to wear when she travels. Thus, if she has several gray suits and likes to wear gray, she buys black luggage.

The luggage is simple, unmarked by any designer or shop. Although the best of its kind, it calls no attention to itself. It is chosen so as not to detract from any of the well-planned elegance of her personal wardrobe and jewelry.

For long trips, the executive woman might buy a large suitcase with wheels on one side and a pull at one end. This allows her to deal with bulk and weight she could never otherwise manage alone. She is able to zip through airports without relying on a stronger person to assist her. Any luggage selected by the successful woman expresses her practical problem-solving point of view.

TRAVEL CLOTHES

Executive women frequently are met at the airport by the people they have arrived to do business with. They therefore plan to arrive already dressed for business. A fine wool gabardine suit reveals its "class" after having been sat in for six hours.

The executive knows which items in her wardrobe arrive looking fresh. If she needs to be ready to travel without more than an hour's notice, she always keeps her staple travel wardrobe fresh and ready to go in her closet. "I can pack for anywhere in the world in less than an hour," boasts a much-traveled executive.

INTERNATIONAL TRAVEL

The executive woman always keeps a valid passport available in case the need for international travel suddenly arises. A passport is convenient to have on hand even if she is traveling to the United States Virgin Islands or Puerto Rico. Although they are U.S. possessions, proof of citizenship is required. An international driving permit along with the driver's license ensures that she can rent a car no matter where in the world she is.

She also keeps handy a small medical kit for medical emergencies. She has small bottles of solutions for diarrhea and intestinal flu, seasickness preventatives, and a few painkillers in case of an accident such as a twisted ankle or a bad case of tennis elbow. She keeps yellow fever and malaria preventives if she has any expectation of traveling to possibly infected areas.

An alarm clock with a night-lighted dial is useful, since the executive is likely to be in many hotel rooms without clocks. She finds it reassuring many time zones away from her home base to know how far she is into the local night. She may elect to keep her clock on home time and her watch on local time as a reference point.

She also takes along packaged snacks or fruit in case she misses a couple of meals or rejects the airline food. "My food staples are apples and baked potatoes," admits a frequent traveler who rejects the processed, chemical-laden food served by the airlines. Another executive routinely packs cheddar cheese.

Trips to the other side of the world are frequently long, grinding flights. If the trip is an overnight flight, the executive woman may take along an athletic sweat suit. After takeoff, she changes to it from her business clothes, which she hangs up overnight. She puts them back on the next morning right before landing. Since she's washed her face and reapplied her makeup too, she arrives looking remarkably refreshed and ready for business.

A device to soothe tense executive nerves is a small tape cassette player-radio and a few tapes of her favorite music. If she plugs in a Vivaldi tape before settling back in her seat with blankets and pillows, the executive can shut out many of the small unfamiliar noises on a flight and improve her chances of a good sleep. The same is true in foreign hotel rooms. "At night in a strange hotel room in New Delhi it's easier to go to sleep listening to my own familiar music," observes another much-traveled woman.

Moreover, having a radio to listen to local stations can be not only interesting and diverting in her hotel room but also a way of keeping abreast of foreign affairs. Further, with a few blank tapes on hand she can dictate notes to have transcribed back at the home office. Note: She travels with plenty of batteries on hand from the U.S. Reliable batteries are harder to find in some other countries.

HOTELS

Executive women stay only at deluxe hotels. It is expected of them by the people they deal with. It reinforces their successful image. Moreover, they take full advantage of the services offered. Overnight laundry service, two-hour dry cleaning, thirty-minute pressing, secretarial services, and other executive services are indispensable to a tired and busy traveler. Massages, gyms and various exercise facilities are relaxing and diverting. In-house beauty salons preclude the necessity of lugging along hair driers and shampoos.

If an executive needs to meet with businessmen in her hotel, she takes a small suite in which the bedroom is a totally separate space. She receives business people in the living room space, having been sure to remove all signs of her personal habitation and to tightly close the doors to the bedroom.

Some hotels provide meeting rooms. These are necessary if the executive is meeting with several people. Her staff arranges for these in advance prior to her arrival to assure their availability.

The traveling woman executive makes full use of room service. If she has no dinner meeting, generally she prefers to eat in her room studying the next day's agenda.

If she goes to the dining room, she speaks to the maître d' to assure that she has a corner table where the light is bright enough to read—and that men diners won't be permitted to bother her.

A good hotel can also offer assistance with local transportation. If a driver and car are needed, the management has an experienced and reliable list. If other transportation is needed the management can arrange for it. In many cities, if requested, the hotel will send a car to pick its guests up at the airport. The executive's staff have checked this out in advance of her arrival so that she knows exactly what to expect.

AIRPORTS

The executive woman has learned that airports can be catagorized into four types.

1. *The large commercial airports that cater to scheduled airlines:* These are all very similar. When she arrives at one of these, she merely follows the signs directing her to the baggage claim area. Car rental counters or local ground transportation such as waiting limousines or taxis are always nearby. Even if she has never been to the airport before, she unerringly heads for her mark.

She also has memberships in all the major airlines' travel clubs. When she has a layover, needs help with her reservations or endures flight cancellations, she goes to the private club accommodations. If there is a long line at the ticket counter, the airline club has a reservations agent who can likely offer the executive friendlier, faster service. Moreover, these clubs have desks and phones from which she can tend to business as necessary. Many of them have television sets, beverages and other amenities.

2. *The small, general aviation airports:* These are airports oriented toward the private, unscheduled aircraft. They are often open during limited hours, with few services late at night. Frequently they lack car rental or taxi services, so the executive pre-arranges for her ground transportation. If open, they always have rest rooms and usually automatic vending machines that sell mostly junk food. Often these airports, which specialize in private aircraft, permit the awaiting car or limousine to drive up to the aircraft door—a special luxury in inclement weather.

3. *The small airports that service both commercial and general aviation:* These are sometimes the most basic facilities, with no guarantee of services. In Third World countries these airports may be closed during the nighttime. They may offer neither food nor water. The toilet facilities may be foul and primitive. The executive woman uses the toilet facilities on her aircraft before disembarking.

4. *The non-airport:* This consists of a strip for landing, perhaps mud or grass, which has absolutely nothing else except maybe a tattered wind sock. There is no building, no personnel, no lights and no tower. The executive woman climbs down from the plane to the ground, gets her luggage out of the side and is completely on her own. She knows this, of course, because she has done her homework. Someone is expecting her and is waiting for her. If not, she probably gets back in the plane and leaves. She has no possibility of contacting anyone from that remote strip.

The executive woman expects things to go wrong when she travels. There are many things that can and do go awry: The rented car is faulty. The hotel has confused her reservations. The plane is late. The flight is canceled. Since she expects things to go wrong, she is calm and resourceful when they do.

She has actively considered ways to facilitate her travel and to simplify it as much as possible. The way she packs, what she takes and the nature of her destination are all part of a deliberate plan. She makes traveling as easy on herself as possible.

WHAT AN EXECUTIVE TRAVELING WOMAN NEVER DOES:

- Carries lots of luggage
- Depends on good skycap service
- Panics when going to a country alone for the first time
- Raises her voice to make sure her English is clear
- Wears a coat and carries a coat
- Overpacks
- Refuses to fly in a small plane or helicopter
- Assumes the water is contaminated in a luxury hotel
- Balks at trying foreign food
- Gets caught in the rain without an umbrella
- Looks for a man to help her carry her luggage
- Fears staying alone in a strange hotel
- Arrives anywhere looking terrible
- Panics when she drives on the left-hand side of the road

9 EXECUTIVE SMALL TALK

Small talk is an important aspect of the executive woman's corporate existence, particularly when she's in that pseudosocial situation known as business entertaining. Her ability to converse at length about virtually *nothing* is a notable asset, and her ability to steer the conversation away from herself is an essential acquired talent.

The executive woman often finds herself in situations with other executives she neither knows well nor wants to know well. She wants to avoid letting any of the specifics of her private life be known.

The exception to this rule is when she is engaged in conversation with the wife of a colleague. Then she may reveal the names of her children and their ages. Other than revealing her devotion to her children, however, she says little about them personally. She does not discuss any problems they may have. She focuses on the more neutral aspects of their lives, e.g., the price of their clothes, video games and what they eat.

Under all circumstances, the achieving woman is reluctant to talk specifically about her job. When she is asked about her responsibilities, the wise woman gives a general view of her job description, since she is likely to be working on projects she does not want broadcast. Moreover, often she finds herself being forced to spend several hours in the company of an executive with whom she is competitive on a project.

At the same time, a woman often has the extra burden of putting her peers at ease. Executive women are more likely to encounter male colleagues who are slightly hostile or who are very uncomfortable with a woman who has attained the responsibilities, success and position that they themselves have. While a woman is prepared to discuss the economic realities of the planet, she does not initiate a profound or conspicuously literate conversation. Her presence is often initially startling to men who are not accustomed to dealing with women as successful as she is. If she conducts a brilliant, witty conversation, she risks being overwhelming.

What does she do? She makes small talk.

Part of the success of the executive woman is due to the fact that she has mastered the art of small talk. She has practiced on her friends until she feels absolutely comfortable talking to anyone anywhere in the world about next to nothing for as long as necessary. She can extend the conversation for hours if necessary. And since she executes the conversation as an art form, no one notices how small the talk really is.

"I really didn't practice small talk on my friends very much," concedes one particularly charming and effective woman. "I practiced on airplanes and anyplace where I could find a captive stranger. I don't think anybody really minded."

While the executive is expanding on the slightest of topics with skill and patience, nothing in her delivery belies that she has conducted a similar conversation at least a hundred times before. Her cheerful demeanor and apparently lively interest camouflage the banality of the conversation.

If she conducts her small talk conversation well, the person she has been talking to will afterward describe her as a pleasant person, intelligent and alert. The person will also be unable to remember exactly what they talked about—"nothing in particular, just things."

The executive woman's priorities are clear: She wants to put the other person at ease.

Toward this end, she adopts several guidelines:

- She concentrates on subjects that are noncontroversial and emotionally neutral.
- She picks subjects of conversation universally experienced.
- She accentuates the positive since positive conversations are more pleasant.
- She carefully avoids criticism and negative statements.

She realizes she knows little of the person she is talking with. Thus the executive woman never makes blanket negative statements such as, "Attorneys drive me crazy. All they do is create busy work and delays." The executive woman has considered the possibility that the person she is talking to adores attorneys, is an ardent fan of the legal profession and is married to an attorney. She stays on the safe and positive side of any subject she discusses.

The executive does not dwell on charities or causes she is involved with. The person she is talking with might get the impression she is soliciting assistance with a heavy hand.

If her life-style is more glamorous than the life of the person she is making small talk with, she is careful not to mention it. Her objective is to make the other person feel positive about the conversation. She steers wide of intimidating people.

She does not dwell on her hobbies or special interests at great length, unless the person she is talking with happens to share them. Most people have little interest in the details of cross-pollenization of roses or in listening for more than two minutes to the joys of sailing.

What does the successful woman small talk about?

- She talks about the weather, since everyone lives in some kind of weather.
- She talks about transportation, since everyone moves from one place to another, even if only from home to the office.
- She talks about food since everyone eats something.
- She talks about inflation since everyone is concerned about inflation.
- She talks about fashion since everyone—at least everyone she deals with in business—wears clothes.
- She talks about electronic gadgetry and computers, since they have become part of life everywhere on the planet.

She reads local papers of any town she is visiting. Local political confrontations and cultural events are always good icebreakers or fillers during an extended conversation. The executive woman's hosts will swell with pride as she compliments their town profusely.

In short, one of the reasons the executive woman is so successful is that she makes people around her feel good. These small talk conversations take place at meals, over cocktails, in taxis, on planes and any time she spends time with someone she doesn't want to know her.

CONVERSATION HIGH POINTS

WEATHER

The executive woman routinely opens her standard small talk conversation by commenting on the weather. She begins, "I know it's boring to talk about the weather, but I must tell you, I've never seen such glorious sunshine," or whatever. She leans forward, turns on a dazzling smile, and is on her way. She takes several tacks.

How It Is Outside Today (Good)

- If it is beautiful, what she would rather be doing than working (gardening, skiing, hiking, running, tennis, golf, sailing).
- That she got up early to enjoy the morning before she went to the office.
- What she intends to do when she finishes working to take advantage of its being such a nice day.
- When it was last so beautiful.
- How much people smile when the sun shines. Nice-people stories ensue.
- How lucky she feels to be here and how unfortunate people in X are today because their weather is awful right now.

How It Is Outside Today (Bad)

- How terrible circumstances bring out the best in people. Stories ensue.
- Stories of blizzards and blackouts ensue. Good Samaritan episodes follow.
- Her worst weather experiences are recounted, compared and contrasted with the other person's.

How the Weather Was Last Week

- How that varies from a year ago.
- Weather patterns. Are they in fact shifting?
- Evidence that the weather is really changing.
- Evidence that the weather is really not changing.
- Are weather patterns behaving uncharacteristically in other parts of the planet?

Growing Up in Weather

- Where she grew up.
- Her life-style as a child because of the climate where she grew up can be compared and contrasted with those of the other person.
- The effects of their childhood climate on their adult tastes, e.g., a passion for skiing from growing up in Minnesota.
- Extremes of the area where the other person now lives are compared and contrasted with the extemes in other areas.

A Discussion of the Current Forecast for the Season

- The lack of reliability of weather forecasting.
- How much money forecasters make. How accuracy does not seem to be a factor in their success.
- Notable instances when forecasters have called it wrong.
- A fantasy forecast. What would you do, how would you feel?

Where the Best and the Worst Weather in the World Is and Why

- Personal preferences are compared and contrasted. (Should the other person's preferences differ from the executive woman's, she expresses admiration for his or her sense of adventure, etc.)
- Florida is compared with Southern California.
- Phoenix is compared with Miami.
- Vermont is compared with Colorado.
- Montana is compared with Utah.

Places Where the Weather is Misunderstood

- Where the weather is supposed to be great—and isn't.
- Where the weather is supposed to be awful—and isn't.
- If the other person has no connection with California, a conversation ensues about how uncertain and often unpleasant weather conditions are in much of California.
- If the other person has no connection with Florida, a discussion of its uncertain climate ensues.
- If the other person has no connection with Oregon, a discussion ensues of what it is like when it rains 300 days a year.

TRANSPORTATION

Streets and Highways

- The deterioration of major metropolitan streets.
- Potholes and bridges.
- The deterioration of interstate highways.
- The outlook for future maintenance of streets and highways.
- Tax possibilities for financing construction and maintenance, e.g., gas taxes, road tolls, truck taxes.

Automobiles

- The prices of cars.
- Which cars perform best.
- Which cars are the best buys.
- The relative values of used American big cars.
- Which cars attract the most attention from police.
- Why Americans can't compete with foreign makers.
- Outlook for big cars.
- Outlook for American cars.
- Mileage efficiency.
- How gasoline costs influenced the buying habits of the executive woman and the other person.
- The cheapest, most practical car to own and operate.
- Whether a $100,000 Rolls-Royce is worth it.
- Fantasy car, the car they've always wanted and never owned.
- Speculations on cars in the 21st century.
- Electronic gadgetry in cars, current and possible future.
- The difficulties of finding reliable car maintenance; rip-offs they have encountered.

Airlines

- Favorite and least favorite airline. Why.
- Stranded airport stories.
- Airport design. They are designed for planes, not people.
- Worst and best designed airport.
- Smallest airport ever flown to.
- Smallest plane ever flown in. Hairiest ride ever taken.
- Worst and best airline food ever eaten.
- Surviving on the cattle car airlines. Stashing food in the briefcase. Stopping en route to the airport to order takeout food.
- Most obnoxious fellow passenger ever encountered.
- How to discourage a fellow passenger from pestering her when she is trying to sleep.
- The airline industry problems and changes.
- Air fares. Lowest and highest. The airline offering the best deal.
- Whether the airlines have succeeded in their courtship of the long-distance automobile driver.

Cruise Ships and Trains

- What kind of cruises are best.
- How do people find time for long cruises? Who goes on them?
- The itinerary of a fantasy cruise.
- Whether trains will be revived as a popular form of vacation travel.
- Whether the Orient Express in Europe is a harbinger of luxury train travel to come. Will we have a luxury train in America?

Mass Transit Systems

- The need for them: pros and cons. Are they the solution for the city of the future?
- Comparisons between existing systems in San Francisco, Montreal, London, Paris and New York.
- The deterioration of the New York subway system.
- Possible funding sources for urban transit.

FOOD

At no point in a discussion about food does the executive woman reveal any personal dietary peculiarities or any medically based dietary adjustments. If she never eats red meat, she never mentions it. If she is a vegetarian, she treats the fact as a private matter. If she is on a low salt diet because she bloats otherwise, she regards that as highly personal information.

Acceptable topics include the following:
- The other person's preferences in restaurants.
- Restaurants in the area where the other person lives.
- Ethnic specialities.
- Favorite restaurant in the United States.
- Favorite restaurant in New York City (which has 22,000!)
- Least favorite restaurant and why.
- Most overpriced restaurant.
- The growth and relative merits of fast food chains.
- Favorite fast food restaurant and why.
- The development of flavored yogurt and popcorn chains.
- The proliferation of cookie stores and ice cream shops.
- Favorite cookie store.
- Which nationality of food would they pick if they could eat only one for the rest of their lives? Italian? Chinese? French? Which one and why.
- Does America have a cuisine of its own? If so, what is it?
- Favorite meals to cook at home. Do they have specialty dishes they prepare?
- Do they keep a garden? If so, what do they grow?
- Places in America with the best availability of fruits and vegetables.
- Favorite supermarkets.
- The merits of winter tomatoes versus summer tomatoes. Why there isn't a good greenhouse tomato.
- The rising costs of food. Specific instances of massive increases in the past decade.

INFLATION

- Which things have increased in price most noticeably over the past five or ten years.
- Whether buying a house this year is a reasonable thing to do. Whether a house purchased today is a good investment.
- Whether the standard of living in the U.S. has gone down. If so, in what areas.
- Outlook for inflation. Will double-digit inflation return?
- Easy ways to save money. Cutbacks in spending.
- The items that cost much less than they did ten years ago: electronic calculators, typewriters, tape cassette players and recorders.

FASHION

A conversation about fashion is usually conducted when the executive woman is meeting with another woman—executive or otherwise. This is not because the executive is discriminating but because many male executives do not shop for themselves and their children. Their wives do this for them.

- Compliments on what the other woman is wearing.
- The exorbitant price of designer clothes.
- The deterioration in quality along with an increase in price in office clothes.
- The high price of handbags.
- Cut-rate drug stores: The wave of the future?
- Whether the stock market does in fact go up and down with hemlines.
- The durability of nonwork clothes. Blue jeans and tennis shoes seem to last forever.

COSMETICS AND BEAUTY

This is a good area for conversing with women who are ill at ease with an executive woman. It is "girl talk," which reveals a side of the executive woman that will put even the most nervous woman at ease.

- Compliment color of nail polish other woman is wearing.
- Discuss brand.
- Whether expensive nail polishes are better than low-priced ones.
- Whether the other woman approves of polish the executive is wearing.
- Discussion of its brand and price.
- Brand names in cosmetics, including favorites.
- Whether the most expensive ones are the best.
- The nature of hype in cosmetic advertising, and its effectiveness.
- Whether new perfumes are superior to the old favorites.
- Favorite perfumes.
- Whether the most expensive perfumes are better or last longer.
- Favorite facial.
- Suggested frequency of facials. Whether they really make a difference.
- Hairdressers: Where the best ones are.
- Whether it is worth it to join a health club.
- Favorite exercise equipment, e.g., Nautilus, and why.
- Whether lifting weights is good for women.
- Exercising with weights.
- Whether health and beauty spas are worth the money.
- Where the best masseuses are.
- Favorite method of massage.

TELEVISION AND ENTERTAINMENT

This conversation is not successful with some managers. The executive woman politely inquires whether the person has any interest in TV or movies. If the response is negative, the achieving woman skips merrily to another topic. The younger the other person is, the likelier it is that this conversation will be a success.

- Favorite TV shows.
- Favorite local newscaster.
- Favorite TV personality.
- Favorite female newscaster.
- Favorite sports event broadcast.
- The sports cable network.
- Impact of cable in general on viewing habits.
- Possible future impact of cable on traditional broadcast television.
- Mini-series: The wave of the future?
- Whether broadcast TV is better than it was five years ago. Why or why not.
- Whether TV is antisocial or a socially bonding agent.
- Whether the other person's children watch TV. How much.
- Betamaxes and TV tape recorders. Whether the person has one or would like to have one. Why.
- New movies. Which ones look interesting.
- Hottest new film stars.
- Favorite old film star.
- Favorite film seen this year.
- Do the Oscars really reward quality or is it all hype?
- Broadway plays—type preferred.
- Broadway plays that look interesting.
- The price of Broadway play tickets.
- Local road show.
- Local theater activities.

COMPUTER-ELECTRONICS

- The penetration of gadgetry into our lives.
- Are video games bad for children?
- Does a child's video game isolate the child from people?
- Are video games any different from watching television?
- New electronic devices recently noted, e.g., telephones with memories, scales that *tell* you how much you weigh, the extent to which microwave ovens are programmed, the number of functions a wristwatch can perform.

- Speculation on what computers can accomplish in the future. The duties they would most like to see a computer take over for them.
- The extent to which their offices are computerized.
- The fantasy office of the future.
- The fantasy home of the future.
- Television printout possibilities. The future of television newspapers.
- Which electronic device they will most likely next purchase?
- The penetration of electronics into other cultures, e.g., a field in remote upper Thailand being plowed by a crude plow and a water buffalo and a farmer alone listening to his portable radio.

All of these conversations are not as routine as first might seem likely, because the executive woman questions her companions, trying to get them to talk about themselves and relax. (She knows that if they can be coaxed into talking about themselves at length, they will remember her cordially.)

Since guests are different, new information is gleaned from each small talk conversation. This the executive woman stores away in her own trove of interesting miscellany.

THINGS THE EXECUTIVE WOMAN NEVER TALKS ABOUT

- Foods she detests
- Places she detests
- People she detests
- Professions she has no respect for
- Problems of her job
- Staff weaknesses
- Health problems she has
- Confidential business information
- What is wrong with her boss
- How much she pays for her clothes
- Her own professional shortcomings
- The biggest boo-boo she ever pulled
- Religion
- Politics
- Ethnic problems
- Sex discrimination
- How superior women are to men
- Whether she colors her hair
- How much money she makes
- Whether she knows how to cook
- Problems with her love life

10 EXECUTIVE
TRAPPINGS

Not only has the executive woman learned to present a successful and powerful appearance through her business wardrobe and grooming; she also knows that certain other trappings underscore her success in the eyes of her colleagues.

Everything from her car to her fountain pen says something positive about her taste, her position and her success. The most effective way for a woman to achieve and maintain status in a men's world is to never let them forget that she is who she is. She does this routinely without having to utter a single word. Her trappings say it all.

JEWELRY

A woman's jewelry makes a strong statement about who she is. What she does not wear says as much as what she does.

The executive woman prefers jewelry that is the real McCoy. She is serious and so are her baubles. (If she owns anything fake, it is a serious copy of the real thing and nobody ever suspects it is not real.) "Even when I was starving and broke I managed to have a few pieces of real jewelry," says one woman who is now able to afford as many pieces as she would like. "My gut just told me that if I *looked* successful I'd increase my chance of being successful."

GOLD VERSUS SILVER

The metal the executive woman prefers is gold. It is a favorite for several reasons. First of all, it is pretty and shiny. Moreover, it is hard for any male colleague to mistake. She may have a diamond or two set in platinum. The diamonds identify their setting as expensive. But when there are not diamonds, the successful woman relies on yellow gold, even though it is less expensive than platinum. Gold is easy to see and has an unmistakable color, whereas platinum, alas, is the color of silver. Executive men see a great deal of silver on their teenage daughters.

If the executive ever wears silver jewelry, it is something special and worthy of comment. The only silver she has ever worn during business hours is a complete earring, necklace and bracelet set by an important designer whose famous work is recognized by the men she deals with—not to mention the women.

Arizona-bred Dr. Dorothy Gregg routinely wears museum-quality silver inlaid Indian jewelry to the boardroom. "Not only is it individual, but it relates to my Western roots," she notes. She knows that men understand its uniqueness.

As mentioned in the chapter on appearance, however, such displays of special accessories must be worn with discretion. Again, the executive woman wants the attention focused on herself, not her jewelry.

PEARLS

After gold, the next most familiar substance donned by the executive woman for adornment is pearl. Since she received her first strand of pearls as a present from her parents when she graduated from high school, she has relied on pearls.

She has two or three basic pearl necklaces. She still owns the little four-millimeter (diameter) strand that her parents gave her when she was sixteen years old. Moreover, she has an opera-length strand that she wears routinely. She also has one long, magnificent strand of nine-millimeter pearls she can wrap around her neck two or three times. This strand may have a splendid gold and diamond clasp on the back, which she wears discreetly resting on the nape of her neck.

(It is generally assumed that the executive woman wears only real pearls. However, it is very difficult for anyone to distinguish the real pearls from the clever fakes.)

Well aware of the pristine reputation pearls have in our society, and also aware that pearls are generally regarded as "ladylike," the executive woman relies on them as a basic accessory. Comments tycoon Mary Eileen O'Keefe astutely, "Pearls have a wonderful pristine connotation, overlaid with images of motherhood and approaching near-Madonnahood. Vicious women simply aren't the ones wearing pearls."

The executive never wears more than three strands at one time during business hours, and she usually wears only one or two. Often she wears pearl earrings with them. "Pearls are the safest jewelry to wear when I'm around clients' wives," observes a sales executive. "I can wear them draped around my neck and there's no jealousy, whereas one little diamond and they're envious."

GEMS

Diamonds are an important accessory for the executive woman. She knows that diamonds are immediately identifiable to her peers. Diamonds cost money. Money means power and success. The executive woman uses diamonds to underscore her success. It is a code immediately interpreted in any boardroom.

How diamonds are presented is of critical importance. Ideally, they are simply mounted. If the diamonds are tiny, then they must be a backdrop for another even rarer, more precious gem of notable size, such as a ruby or an emerald—something easily identifiable. Small diamonds set in a cluster by themselves are not as impressive.

The executive knows that with diamonds the whole is infinitely more valuable than the sum of its parts. The bigger the diamonds, the more valuable they are. "If I was going to wear something fake, I'd wear a large fake diamond, set in 18-carat gold," divulges a chic executive. "Since everything else I wear is real, people assume the diamond is real too."

BRACELETS

For business, the executive relies on a gold bracelet. It is simple and appropriate for many different occasions. She may wear the same gold bracelet every day. (After all, gold does not wear out.) She never wears silver bracelets unless she collects rare and noticeably exquisite silver bracelets.

If she wears a jeweled bracelet in the daytime, it is adorned with a simple colored stone, exquisitely yet simply set.

EARRINGS

Earrings are a basic accessory the executive woman routinely wears. Whether or not her ears are pierced is not important. What is important is that the earrings are simple and do not detract from her face. They may be simple pearl earrings or simple, unadorned, multicarat diamond earrings. She also wears gold earrings simply designed in the shape of a fan or knot.

Dangling earrings are rejected as being too frivolous.

The only fake earrings she owns are gold-plated copies of ancient gold earrings fashioned after lions' heads in the Metropolitan Museum of Art. She knows the history of the originals and explains to anyone who notes her earrings. She also knows that the originals in gold are too heavy to be worn practically on her ears.

NECKLACES

Thin gold chains never enter into the executive suite. The executive woman never wears several thin chains (including those with small initials and figures on them). She knows they are popular with junior employees who cannot afford one really heavy gold necklace. Regardless of length, any gold necklace the executive woman wears around her neck is substantial. She is well aware that when she wears it she is in effect presenting it as a credential. Thus she would much prefer to go unadorned than to wear something of little consequence near her face.

She may on occasion wear an antique locket or a jeweled pendant—it is, of course, impressive, interesting or exquisite.

One of the most effective pieces of jewelry is a simple pendant adorned with one sizable diamond. It rests on a gold chain high on her throat. The setting matches similar earrings, and the effect is one of pure elegance.

PINS AND BROOCHES

The executive woman uses these items to personalize an otherwise plain outfit. She has an antique diamond stickpin for her lapel. She wears a pearl and diamond brooch to hold a drape on a white silk blouse. She has several pieces of Victorian jewelry she wears decoratively to personalize her routine appearance. "After all, I don't want to look like I was pressed out of a cookie cutter," says one executive who uses an inherited assortment of brooches to enliven her "uniform."

RINGS

The executive woman is particularly sensitive about what rings she wears. "After taking out the time every week to get a manicure, I don't want to wear any ordinary ring," observes one high-ranking woman. "If the ring is not exquisite and special, I won't wear it." Generally, silver rings and rings set with pearls and semiprecious stones are not considered appropriate.

Unless rings are a matched set designed to be worn together, no more than three rings should be worn on the hands at a given time. Important rings lose their impact when many are worn simultaneously.

Diamond rings are most powerful, and as a general rule, rings representing animals, objects or flowers are less powerful than simpler arrangements. They are too frivolous to be executive.

The executive also gives thought to the placement of the rings on her hands. Generally, she wears rings on the third and fourth fingers. Thus when she shakes hands no ring intrudes into the handshake. Any ring for her small finger is carefully chosen so as not to injure a hand offered in an enthusiastic handshake.

Moreover, rings worn on the index fingers are generally designed for dinner wear instead of the office.

WATCHES

The one essential piece of jewelry an executive woman wears is her watch. It is an indispensable part of her image.

She wears a simple gold watch with a dark strap. Importantly, the watch has an identifiable, upscale manufacturer whose name is written clearly on the dial. This is the only signature the executive woman would ever consider wearing. "I don't flaunt it. But I have lots of opportunities to flash it when someone asks what time it is," notes an executive woman.

The aluminum and gold watches that have been recently popular are too sporty for the executive suite. And the executive woman, unless she works on the West Coast, which is usually more casual, prefers a gold watch with a plain leather band over a gold watch with a gold band for the office. She saves her glittery watch for evening wear.

FURS

It is perfectly acceptable for an important woman to dress in an elegantly cut dark cloth coat. No matter how cold it is outside, furs are not really critical for her image.

However, when a woman does choose a fur, she is careful to select the right one.

Mink is the perfect coat worn by executive women—dark mink, simply and classically cut. Men and women everywhere respond positively to its statement about a woman's success.

A matching mink hat makes a very effective entrance to meetings. The hat comes off when the coat does. Although mink is flattering to most faces, if a woman wears a hat after the men remove their hats, it weakens her presence by underlining her femininity. Since she will whip it off before she goes into the meeting, she wears a hat that looks elegant without wrecking her hair.

The executive woman who does not own a mink coat and wears a fur coat to the office opts for a very dark raccoon coat and hat. Once again, the dark fur is very powerful.

In either case the fur coat is richly lined, and has luxurious fittings and her initials embroidered inside.

Interestingly, mink and raccoon coats are reasonably good investments, since both furs shed very little and if cared for endure for decades.

An executive woman would never wear a fun fur; rabbit, monkey, kangaroo, and foxtails are out. Further, antique furs are for young junior assistants. "I would never wear a long fur dyed a strange color. It would dilute my image," notes one powerful woman.

A fine silver fox or lynx fur is beautiful, but neither has the impact of a fine dark fur. Fur capes, stoles and wraps have no place in the executive woman's corporate wardrobe. Short mink jackets lose the impact of a full-length coat. The executive prefers a well-cut cloth coat instead.

CARS

The executive woman recognizes that a car is a further extension of the image she projects. If she drives to work and has an assigned space at the office parking lot, she knows that colleagues connect her car with their image of her.

First of all, her car is well groomed. Grooming for a car consists of washing, vacuuming, cleaning and tip-top maintenance. At no time is there litter left in the car from a weekend trip to the lake, because an executive never knows when she may want to drive a colleague to lunch in order to sway the colleague to her point of view on an issue.

The car she chooses must enhance her executive image. She has just the right make, the right color and the right style so that when other executives see her car for the first time they think, "Of course."

The age of the automobile is not important as long as it is in immaculate condition and running order. Vintage cars, however, are not part of the executive image. They are for weekends and her nonbusiness private life. The executive wants her business car to reflect her businesslike attention to detail and performance.

An executive who deviates from driving the generally acceptable executive type of car does so with conscious flair. One grandmother who is a long-established senior executive drives a gray Ferrari with black leather

AUTOMOBILES

JUST RIGHT	TOO FLASHY	TOO MUNDANE	TOO CHEAP	TOO TACKY
Mercedes sedan	Any convertible	Any station wagon	Volkswagen	Jeep
Mercedes sedan diesel	Eldorado Cadillac	Dodge	Mustang	Van
Jaguar sedan	Lotus	Chevrolet	Economy cars	Pickup
BMW	Corvette	Pontiac		Edsel
Cadillac Seville	De Lorean	Buick		
Porsche	Ferrari	Thunderbird		
Rolls-Royce				
Limousine				
Volvo				
Firebird				
Aston-Martin				

upholstery. She admits that her secure entrenchment as a longtime high-ranked employee helped her get the courage to drive it. "I probably wouldn't have driven a Ferrari ten years ago—I couldn't have afforded it either," she observes.

"In today's world, I think a big gas guzzler would be bad for my image," opines a highly ranked woman in the banking industry. "I want to look successful—not wasteful." She drives a navy BMW.

The color of the car is generally brown, navy blue, black, gray, beige or cream. The executive women does not even consider buying a loud yellow, red, pink, orange, green or turquoise car. Generally, executives prefer standard license numbers on their cars, feeling that vanity plates are too flashy.

ACCESSORIES

An executive woman extends her sense of style and taste to include often-used items around her. Whether it is the antique clock on her desk or the date book she whips out, every aspect of her presence has been carefully selected.

She shops for her accessories in places where her male colleagues shop for their wives. This makes it easy for her male counterparts to acknowledge a Hermes or Ferragamo scarf even though the signature is never exposed. Likewise, her gold pen is from a famous Fifth Avenue shop, as is her simple leather pocketbook. If she smokes, her lighter is a gold Dunhill.

Nowhere, however, except for her watch, does the executive woman wear a signature, identifying stripe or logo. She expresses her success with a subtle elegance. She leaves signatures and initials for women who are less secure and who feel a need to tell people where they shop. The executive woman communicates her success with consummate understatement.

HER OFFICE

The executive woman's office clearly defines her rank in her company. "An office is like a title," says an executive whose spacious quarters overlook New York harbor. "It's no fun to make a fuss about it, but it is important. Your title impresses the men outside your company. It's portable. You take it with you on your business card. Your office impresses the men inside your company."

"Women who are reluctant to make a fuss about their offices are dumb," declares another. "The executive office should clearly say she has made it."

Typically, it is a corner office with several windows along two walls. It is spacious. To reach it, one or more secretaries and assistants must be passed. The more people who must be passed to reach her, the more powerful the executive is.

Her office furniture is grouped into two or three distinct areas. Her desk is in one corner of the room, with two facing chairs. In another corner is a sitting area with couches and a couple of low tables and upholstered chairs. This is the most informal corner of the room, where she frequently sits with cohorts for informal discussions. There is a telephone with several lines on a table near the couch sitting area, as well as on her desk. She may light the office with lamps instead of typical overhead office lights, enhancing its relaxed mood.

In another corner is a conference table with four chairs around it—optional if her office adjoins a separate conference room with a larger table and six to ten chairs around it. Sometimes a suite of executive offices contains one or two conference rooms that are shared by all of the executives on that floor.

The executive woman has original framed artwork hanging on her walls—another company-provided perk that reflects her good taste and judgment. If she has a special interest in art, she hangs something from her personal collection on her wall. If she chooses to include pictures of her family, they are elegantly framed. Small sculptures, industry awards and civic acknowledgments are the chief objects on the credenza behind her desk and on the tabletops. She also uses sports trophies and work-related items as bookends in her bookcase. A small tree or a large, dense plant potted in an interesting pot stands in a corner.

Generally, her office is indistinguishable from those of her male peers.

One acknowledgment of her femininity may be her choice of fabric. Whereas a male counterpart may opt for big, dark leather chairs, she probably selects lighter colors and textured fabrics. Further, she has one or two flower arrangements in the office. The arrangements are exquisite; the flowers are unusual and interesting.

In short, someone who visits her has no question as to her power and authority. "When I want to get the upper hand, I try to get someone to come and see me in my lair," says a woman whose office is decorated with fine art and antiques. "When they see all this they know I must be doing something right."

TRAPPINGS NEVER SEEN ON EXECUTIVE WOMEN OR IN THEIR OFFICES

- Designer signatures and initials and stripes
- Diamond bracelets
- Dangling earrings
- Multiply pierced ears with several earrings in each ear
- Trite silver jewelry
- Thin gold chains
- Cocktail rings
- Rings with dangling hearts

- Initials in gold or diamonds
- Monograms
- Bangle bracelets
- Charm bracelets
- Identification bracelets
- Costume jewelry
- Fun furs—rabbit, mouton
- Silver rings
- Bic lighters
- Pearl rings
- Nylon scarves
- Ankle bracelets
- Posters
- Metal furniture
- Small green plants in plastic pots
- Snapshots in a plastic cube
- Piles of paper and magazines
- Typewriters
- File cabinets
- Carnations, mums or gladiolas
- Clutter
- Hanging plants
- A valentine from her four-year-old child

PART THREE

ON HER OWN TIME: AFTER-HOURS, WEEKENDS AND HOLIDAYS

Not all of an executive's time away from the office is leisure time. Part of the definition of "executive" seems to be that the hours spent working are often without limit. Whenever she is working, whether at lunch or dinner, at an industry meeting or a corporate meeting at a resort, the executive woman is careful to act precisely in character with the powerful, competent image she wants to project.

She does not have the luxury of being able to collapse, either when she is home with a miserable flu or worse, in the hospital. When business intrudes, she is almost always able to pull her act together on a second's notice.

Still, she has programmed some time into her life for herself—although it never seems to be enough. She takes time to stay fit and attractive. She takes time to keep healthy. And she finds a retreat somewhere for herself. It may be a quiet room in the attic with a "Do not disturb" sign on the door that her family respects. Or it may be a special quiet place in the country. It may be at home at six in the morning when she gets up to bathe, dress, feed and coo intimately to her two-year-old daughter.

Almost nothing in the life of an executive women is random. Every act is planned. Every minute is planned. Even fun and sleep are planned. It has to be that way.

11 IS
HER LIFE
HER OWN?

The executive woman has a very clear view of how she wants to be perceived by her peers, her boss and her corporate hierarchy. If she reports to the head of a major company, she is aware of how carefully she is observed by her peers at the other companies in her industry across the country and by other executives in her community.

CLUBS, CIVIC AFFAIRS AND HOBBIES

The executive woman knows that the clubs and civic and national affairs she associates herself with affect how she is perceived by all those watching her progress. She carefully considers both the positive and negative aspects of a commitment to live in one place over another or to interact with people in a particular club or organization.

The size of the community she lives in becomes an important factor in her choices. "If you live and work in the same town as your boss, your boss's interests can be a vital factor in your decision about which civic organizations you are involved with," notes one executive woman. The smaller the town, the more restricted a woman's options are. Thus, if a woman is not wedded to her boss's life-style and feels she has as much exposure to her boss as she wants or needs during her working hours, she may elect to move to an adjacent community away from constant contact with other company employees. There she will have more freedom in her evening activities at the clubs and restaurants she frequents without factoring in contact with her superior.

By the same token, if she feels she does not get enough senior attention, her choices are simple. She investigates her boss's interests and claims that his or her favorite activities are her own favorites. She finds out which clubs her boss frequents and joins them enthusiastically. Chances are she will then get important new attention.

However, the price of this kind of attention is that an executive's private life will be considerably diminished, since when she is involved in *anything* with her superiors she is, in essence, working. Any contact that reflects back on her professional life and career involves her public self. "Whenever I'm doing anything the head of the company will hear about, you better believe I consider that working," observes one successful woman who avoids memberships that entail after-hour corporate contact. "I'm already successful. I want my private life too," she says.

Clubs can be a positive experience for the young executive honing her professional skills. "You can get experience in managing a professional organization long before you have an opportunity to manage so large a production in the office. You get practice managing and you learn more about handling people," notes Dr. Dorothy Gregg.

When the executive woman joins professional clubs, she is careful to select some that include both men and women in the membership. However, she also belongs to one or two specifically women's organizations that discriminate against men—just as some men belong to exclusively male organizations. "Maybe we'll create our own specifically female power network and cease to feel so excluded from the old boy clubs," comments one female executive.

"I pick a club that gives me access to other successful executives who probably encounter similar problems," notes a senior fashion executive. "Clubs help me with my job. When I run into some new decision I have not previously encountered, I can call up someone I know who runs a similar company and ask how he or she has dealt with the problem. Since they are my equals I don't mind admitting when I haven't the slightest idea what route to take in my decision making."

The executive woman should carefully weigh the pros and cons of joining professional organizations related to her work. For instance, if she is an attorney she should consider carefully whether she wants to become active in the leadership of local legal organizations. "If you fail in public in an organization, it has a ripple effect throughout your entire community of peers," notes one executive. "So you don't fail. It's that simple. You just never fail." Attaining a highly visible position in professional organizations can backfire. Unforeseen issues can sometimes become emotionally charged and the leadership is placed in a no-win situation.

Some successful women opt out of professional organizations. "I am asked to speak at them all the time," observes a prominent executive. "But I was never a member of those things." Another woman agrees. "I pay my dues and show up once a year. But I refuse to take any active role."

It is important for the executive woman to avoid organizations that are perceived as radical or controversial by the mainstream of her business community. For instance, it would be political suicide for a woman executive with a forest products firm to join an organization opposed to cutting trees, or for an executive with a drug company that makes birth control products to speak out in favor of the nonmedical "rhythm method."

"I've always taken my cue on memberships from the level of management above me," candidly admits a successful broadcast executive. "If they joined, I joined. If they didn't, I didn't. It was simple and it seems to have worked," she smiles.

Most often, the successful woman belongs to organizations that reflect the interests of her private life but are not detrimental in any possible way to her professional profile.

The successful woman cultivates her hobbies. Thus, a product manager is active in a wildlife organization that sponsors trips into wilderness areas to observe wildlife. An attorney is an underwater photographer. Another executive with a consumer products company is an avid sailor. A mergers and acquisitions specialist raises hybrid roses. A peripatetic accountant is an avid bird watcher, taking along her field glasses wherever she goes. Pursuing hobbies in her spare time gives an executive an outlet, and also, importantly, contributes to her dimensions as a person. "It adds one more string to your bow," says one woman.

GOAL CAUSES

It is also important for women executives to become active in charity. For instance, a California-based television executive is on the board of a deaf clinic in Los Angeles as well as a local theater company. The theater company provides an important outlet for new plays and connects with her work in television. "I told them I can't make the lunches but I will do what I can to help," says the busy executive, who is also a wife and mother.

Charity work often increases an executive woman's access to other executives in her own company and in her community. While she is in a situation to accomplish genuine good for her community, she can also raise her visibility in the local newspapers by heading up a fund-raising dinner or outing for the organization. Moreover, she has an excuse to telephone executives with whom she otherwise has little contact to solicit their support. She gets their attention—all in the name of doing good for the cause. Both the organization and the woman executive benefit.

Museums are prime examples of other good causes that provide the public with important cultural experiences and the executive with a popular cause.

Organizations Where It Is Hard To Lose

• Museums
• Libraries
• Colleges

- Public radio and television stations
- Hospitals
- Symphony companies
- Opera companies
- Ballet companies
- Major disease-fighting organizations such as the American Cancer Society
- Girl Scouts
- Charity foundations to help the needy
- Civic restoration projects
- The Audubon Society
- Scholarship committees for talented needy youths
- Impoverished neighborhood self-help projects
- Hierarchy of traditionally acceptable religious institutions

EXECUTIVE RESIDENCE

The executive woman picks where she lives with the same care as she picks her affiliations. She under no circumstances has the only nice house in a bad neighborhood—unless she is in the forefront of an urban rehabilitation organization, generally a gesture commended by the business community. Chances are the executive lives in a prestigious, elegant part of town in a house or apartment generally admired by her colleagues.

The executive woman has learned it is far better to have a tiny house in the best part of town than a big house in the worst part of town. The same goes for a tiny co-op in the finest building rather than cavernous quarters in a questionable building.

When a woman makes it to the top, she may consider it important to telegraph her colleagues that she is there. Since her value to her corporation is underlined by the compensation it pays her, a woman has to be doubly careful to leave no doubt that she is indeed valued by her organization.

Unfortunately, frequently male observers may try to detract from her worth. The executive woman has learned to underscore her success. Where she lives is one method.

EXECUTIVE VACATIONS AND COUNTRY HOUSES

The woman executive picks her vacations and weekend retreats or summer houses with the same care she uses to choose her civic and cultural affiliations.

If she wants to make a bigger impression on her boss and he loves his vacation house on St. John in the Virgin Islands, she may want to visit that island on her vacation. Thus she has used her vacation to open a possibly important new communication line. If she knows he always has a summer house in Southhampton, Long Island, she rents one nearby for the summer (or a month) and occasionally runs into him since, after all, they know many of the same people.

Conversely, if she feels confident of the attention she routinely receives in her organization, she uses her vacations and holidays to escape and to add new dimensions to her life. Whether she vacations in Nepal trekking at the base of Mt. Everest or charters a boat sailing off Fiji, her unusual experiences enhance her image. They also give her a fresh perspective that may make her more effective on her job. She not only enjoys herself enormously but brings back fresh conversation and a wealth of new observations to make small talk more interesting with her colleagues when they are on a trip together to London or Des Moines.

Most executive women find their weekends are more essential to their emotional well-being than their vacations. Successful women restore their energy and perspective by escaping to a house—no matter how simple it may be—in the country. Even if week-long holidays are rare, the long weekend isn't. "I pack up the kid and my husband and we go to our house. I work there too, but it seems totally different. We get up at 5 A.M. Monday mornings and I return to my real life ready to go at it again," describes a Los Angeles wonder woman.

The working woman who is the most successful recognizes the amount of stress in her life as wife, mother and executive. She has learned to value herself; she literally gives herself a break. She has learned that taking time out to relax is worth it. A single hour walking alone in the woods can undo much of the stress generated in a week of never-ending responsibility. She carves times out for herself to recharge her much-drained battery.

12 EXECUTIVE HEALTH AND MAINTENANCE

Not only does the successful woman accommodate herself by planning weekend escapes from the mental stress and strain, she also nurtures her physical self.

She is aware of the psychological impact her vitality and energy have on her peers, underlings and clients. By appearing ready to take on any endeavor, no matter how mentally draining and physically taxing, she seems more powerful.

EXECUTIVE HEALTH HABITS

The woman at the top has learned that health is equated with capability and that sickness is weakness. Maintaining her health and sense of well-being are important aspects of the executive's life-style.

The executive woman wants to glow with vitality and well-being. She has shiny, healthy, clean hair, bright eyes and a clear complexion. She is fit, trim, firm and toned and moves around the corporate rooms with obvious energy.

She works at it. Whether she likes it or not, she is subject to a double standard: She *has* to be fit. She has to be trim. Whether it means getting up at dawn to do calisthenics or working out at the Y during lunch, the executive woman is forced to adopt a life-style that keeps her healthier than many of her male colleagues.

The achieving woman has personal health habits that engender the best possible health consequences. She sleeps well and adequately. She believes in and practices preventive medicine. She is on close terms with her physician in order to enable her to arrange medical appointments without disrupting her schedule or calling attention to the appointments.

If she is very lucky, she works at a company that sponsors in-house fitness programs. Some forward-looking companies have built their own executive gyms to try to encourage their personnel to stay fit. If there is a gym in her company, she participates actively in the program. Many other companies have co-sponsored gyms near their headquarters. For instance, there are cardio-fitness centers in Houston and on Wall Street in New York that a number of corporations banded together to build.

By adopting a healthy life-style, the successful woman is one step up on her less fit male and female colleagues when she arrives at a meeting. Not only does she look great, but she really feels good. The better she feels, the clearer becomes her thinking and the more quickly she can make accurate analyses and judgments.

Moreover, executive women are less likely than men to smoke—another health plus. One recent study indicates that two-thirds of the women executives never smoke, compared to 59 percent of the men. The same study shows that 13 percent of the women use tranquilizers compared to 12 percent of the men. This indicates that despite all the added burdens placed on her, the executive woman is a coping woman who has her complicated act remarkably together.

The successful woman's corporate survival instinct prompts her to compensate for any weakness she may have. So the worse she feels, the more attention she pays to her appearance. It may require eye drops to clear her eyes, but she arrives for her meeting bright-eyed and bushy-tailed no matter what it takes. Moreover, she uses color to compensate for a pale complexion or sallow skin. She puts to good use a woman's prerogative to wear more color in the office. The day the sky is gray and she feels awful, she shows up in a pink blouse and lipstick with circles under her eyes carefully camouflaged under makeup. If she feels terrible, she wears a red scarf in the neck of her black suit. She knows the red will reflect warmly on her sallow face.

THE FLU

Moreover, the executive woman has learned to work well even when she doesn't feel well. She is careful not to complain when she has a headache or feels fluish.

A New York sales executive wife and mother says, "When I don't feel good, nothing is different in my schedule. My life is too complex to try to move things around. Maybe I can cancel lunch here and there and spend a weekend in bed. Basically when I don't feel good the only difference in my work is that I do it feeling pretty awful."

"I try not to lose perspective when I feel terrible," says another executive. "When I feel I'm losing my objectivity, I sit in my office alone for a few minutes, tell my secretary to hold my calls, close my eyes and think of what the sunset looks like viewed from the back porch of my country house."

When she is simply too sick to manage to drag her body into her office, the executive is careful that her secretary does not reveal that she is infirm.

"She is out of the office right now," the secretary tells any caller. "Can I have her call you?" Since the executive is in constant touch with her staff, she can return important calls without giving a clue that she is running a 103-degree temperature and bedridden. "I merely say I am not in my office at the moment if my client asks me about some matter I don't have in front of me to reference. They think I've never been sick a day in my life," confides one sales executive. If she ducks out home to bed for an afternoon, her secretary reports to callers that she is in a meeting for the rest of the day. No responsible executive is ever too sick to return important calls. Her staff does not telegraph her illness. Other executives are informed only if they ask. Only her boss is routinely notified.

EXECUTIVE STEADINESS

Importantly, the executive woman furnishes no evidence for the macho stereotype about women being influenced by their menstrual cycles. She is careful to keep her own supply of sanitary napkins and tampons—so no curious clerk sees her buying one in the ladies rest room only to report later, "No wonder Mrs. Smith is such a terror today; she's having her period."

Aware of the mythology women have been burdened with in regard to being influenced intellectually by their bodily rhythms, she is careful to keep hers a complete mystery. Under no circumstances does she cry or become overwrought and emotional, regardless of the circumstances. The stereotype of a hysterical woman is one that the executive woman is constantly up against. She is unwaveringly cool as a cucumber, even-tempered and predictable.

Interestingly, successful working women are the least likely category of women to experience negative biological and psychological problems during menopause. (A recent study shows housewives are the most likely to experience negative symptoms.)

HOSPITAL STAYS

When it is necessary for a woman executive to undergo surgery, she and her staff keep it quiet. Since her secretary is continually in touch with the hospitalized executive, most of her colleagues are under the impression she is out of town on business. So are all casual inquirers. Business continues as normal. Avoiding disruption of business diminishes the impact of an executive's absence from the office. If there is no announcement of ill health, she continues to be perceived as a very healthy person.

Should she require prolonged hospitalization, the woman executive over-achieves again. One successful woman recalls, "My doctor found an abdominal tumor that required immediate surgery. He wanted to put me in the hospital the same day. I said not until tomorrow afternoon. I spent the next morning getting my roots colored and doing my calisthenics—I knew it would be weeks before I could do either of those things. I checked into the hospital at 3 P.M. with a valise full of beautiful silk robes and two briefcases full of office work. He operated on Friday and on Monday I was giving dictation to my secretary." As always, the executive woman pays attention to details. She takes care to look as attractive as possible in anticipation of visitors from the office. She wants to be the healthiest-looking sick person her staff and her boss have ever seen.

It's this kind of extra effort that made the woman executive so successful in the first place.

The woman executive gives no clue as to uterine difficulties, breast tumors, Fallopian tube procedures or any other specifically feminine medical or surgical treatments. Should she have a mastectomy, she might instead claim gall bladder surgery—accounting generally for the nature of the bandaging to any curious visitor from the office. (By the same token, a male executive is not going to let it be known that part of his prostate was removed.)

The woman executive has learned that by avoiding publicity about medical problems related to her sexuality she deprives any male detractors of some cannon fodder to shoot her down.

Serious Health Problems

The female executive is in the same boat as her male colleagues when it comes to cancer-related surgery. There is much misunderstanding about the treatment of cancer. Admitting its discovery can be an impediment to a promotion or added responsibilities because of hysteria sometimes aroused by the mere suggestion of a malignancy.

If the woman executive has a small malignant stomach tumor removed, she only mentions the fact that it was a small stomach tumor. She denies there was any complication. Any cancer preventive program she undertakes is described merely as "treatment of continuing intestinal problems—nothing serious."

Another area in which women suffer from a prejudice about future capability on their job is heart problems. Like her male counterparts, a woman who experiences chest pains and subsequent hospitalization may label it as a bout of gall bladder to everyone at the office. She knows that just as there is little understanding of the nature of recovery from malignancy, so there is a phobia about heart disease.

The woman executive has to be more secretive about any of her physical problems than her male counterparts because women have to counteract male prejudice about their "emotionalism." Thus, if a male executive has part of his prostate removed, his emotional aftermath is not as closely observed and noted by his colleagues as a woman who has her uterus removed. "Old lady Smith is having hormonal problems. Did you see how excited she was when Allen botched that proposal?" is a conceivable comment that might be made about a woman. Also, it's made behind her back, where she has no opportunity for rebuttal.

THERAPY

The prejudices against women as executives have made it imperative for them to present themselves as bastions of sanity, togetherness and mental calm. Very often one of the few people they can confide in is a psychiatrist. "Women executives are under exceptional pressure," notes one physician. "Her psychiatrist may be one of the few outlets she can honestly open up to."

Far be it that any word of mental help should escape into the corporate suite. "I pay for my shrink out of my own pocket, even though my health insurance covers it. I don't want it anyplace on file in the company," says one executive who has a long-time relationship with a therapist. She is aware of the fact that her visibility as the only senior vice president in her conservative company's history makes her far too vulnerable to innuendo and rumor. It is worth the extra money for her to be assured that her visits to her psychiatrist are strictly in confidence.

Other executives feel more comfortable about processing their psychotherapy treatment bills through their company's insurance department. It depends on the nature of the company and the visibility—and the vulnerability—of the woman in question.

The savvy executive is well aware of the limelight focused on her. She knows that her presence in the executive ranks continues to be denigrated as tokenism by some of her detractors. She is always mindful of this when she files a medical insurance claim.

COSMETIC SURGERY

A claim she will never file is one for cosmetic surgery, such as a face-lift or eye area tuck. The woman executive is aware of the youth cult in America, and like some of her male peers, she sneaks off to have her face repaired as needed. She does this on vacation and in a city where there is a beauty spa. After the surgery, she checks in at the spa. She admits going to the spa but not having the surgery. "Boy, that spa really did a world of good for Mrs. Smith," notes a particularly observant and dim-witted staff member when she returns looking refreshed and unusually relaxed. Mrs. Smith is quick to praise the merits of the spa she visited.

Cosmetic surgery is an alternative the executive woman candidly considers in private. If she inherited bags under her eyes that give her a tired, morose look, she may have them removed. If she inherited any unseemly facial characteristic, she considers altering it. She has no intention of looking like Barbie doll, but she understands the vulnerability of successful women in the office. While conventional plastic beauty is not a concern or ideal held by the achieving woman, she is aware of the double standards imposed upon her. Any physical deformity or unsightliness will be used very cruelly against her and may impede her upward progress.

After she is in her forties, the ambitious woman takes a close look at herself. She knows that obvious aging will be used more harshly against her than it will her male counterparts. When they are "seasoned veterans of the corporate arena," she is an "old lady ready for pasture" in their perceptions.

If she feels that she is aging quickly and that it is detrimental to her future, every couple of years she consults a highly reliable and recommended plastic surgeon who is not "knife happy" to determine when she will substantially benefit from a nip here and a tuck there. When she feels like she needs a repair, she has it—on vacation time. Moreover, facial massage is something she incorporates into her hectic schedule as a necessary luxury. With scrupulous attention to skin care and massage, she prolongs her skin's freshness and elasticity.

SUMMING UP: THE APPROPRIATE EXCUSE

The executive woman gives the people she works with as few excuses as possible to not take her seriously. She is never "sick," "ailing" or "ill." She is occasionally "slightly indisposed." The woman executive has learned that if she must be indisposed, some reasons are much more acceptable than others.

Negative Executive Ailments	Acceptible Executive Ailments— Complaints Men Use
Headache	Sinus
Menstrual cramping or discomfort	Minor ulcer flare-up
Breast tumor	Gall bladder problems
Uterine problems	Hemorrhoids
Abortion or early miscarriage	Sprained back
Cosmetic surgery	Dental surgery
Tubes tied—Fallopian surgery	Tonsilectomy or Appendectomy
Insomnia	Arthritis—tennis elbow kept her from sleeping
Urethritis	Ulcers again
Emotional stress	Tennis elbow
Cancer therapy	Root canal work
D & C	Mole excised from her back
Diarrhea	Intestinal problems

13 CORPORATE
FAMILY
LIFE

The woman executive who has a family has an added burden few successful men have ever faced. Nine out of ten male executives have full-time wives at home to run their homes and manage their children. These executives' wives see that the house is clean, get the children to school, attend PTA meetings, plan the menus and take care of the laundry. They are a valuable asset to their husbands, permitting these hardworking men to focus solely on getting the job done at the office.

The woman executive, alas, has no wife. She is her own support system. The woman who competes daily against men in the traditional men's world— the office place—is at a disadvantage from the time she gets up to begin her work day. She is unlikely to have the luxury of focusing solely on getting her office job done. She has her other jobs to juggle as well. Like the wives of her male colleagues, she manages the house, cares for the children and plans the menus. If she has a husband he no doubt expects the traditional wifely services to be administered to him, such as preparing dinner, replacing missing buttons, ironing, and acting as hostess when entertaining his clients. These add to the personal responsibilities of the female executive.

The woman who juggles a career at the top of the male-dominated corporate world has, at the very least, to do for herself all the things that wives do for their husbands. If she has a husband, her duties expand to include his needs. If she has children, her total responsibilities are incredible. "Motherhood changed my priorities," observes a television executive. "I have more priorities now—and unfortunately none of them are me personally. I'm very conscious of organization in my life. I am much more organized than I ever dreamed possible. I used to lunch with friends occasionally. No more. I work through lunch every day so my chances of getting out of the office at a reasonable hour are better and maybe I can get home before my daughter's bedtime."

The executive woman is usually able to hire someone to help her with the housework and her children. With luck she also gets assistance from her husband and other family members. In a pinch she asks friends to lend a hand. But even with many helping hands she still accepts the responsibilities for myriad aspects of her non-business life.

Part of the reason she tends to accept the lion's share of household and family responsibility is in her own psychology. The overachieving woman who succeeds in business may be unlikely to admit she cannot be all things to all people. She is often reluctant to ask for help or to delegate as much as she could if she were not so determinedly overachieving. She tries to do it all herself.

Thus, she is the one who inventories the groceries and the toiletries and is most concerned with preparing the meals. She is the one who buys and repairs her children's clothes and usually the one who decorates and oversees the house. She gives parties for her children's birthdays and dinners for her husband's business associates.

Executive, wife and mother. We have in our midst our own race of superwomen. These women are not likely to complain. Somehow, they cope.

EXECUTIVE LIFE SUPPORT SYSTEM

The essence of the life of the corporate woman is organization. Since she has no wife support system, she makes lists of groceries, lists of repairs, lists of menus, and daily checklists of her other lists. She organizes errands by category as well as by physical proximity. She has a clear sense of her priorities and constantly sifts out the essential from the inconsequential. She accepts the fact that many little things will simply never be done. Her life is simplified down to its basics.

THE HOUSEKEEPER

The successful woman often rents a wife. "The support system is the housekeeper," declares Elaine Linker. While the housekeeper can look after the children and do some of the shopping, many personal responsibilities still rest on the corporate woman's shoulders. She still makes up the menus and coordinates the schedules of any other family members. She decorates the house and dresses the family. She drops her shoes off at the repair shop and orders bed linens. She calls the refrigerator repairman and replaces the lawn furniture. She calls the butcher from her office. "I spend a lot of money on services," notes another New York executive. "Cleaning, delivering, picking up, baby-sitting, and the housekeeping. A woman can't do this if she doesn't make a lot of money. If I were not a success it just wouldn't be worth it."

THE SHOPPING

One corporate president has finally given up doing the routine grocery shopping herself, even though she did a better job than her housekeeper. "No more. The staff buys it," she says. "When we don't have what we want or what we prefer we do without it until the staff has time to buy whatever we lack. If the roast beef is a poor cut, I don't feel guilty that I didn't pick it out. I could have bought a poor cut too."

Maintaining her wardrobe is an added burden for the executive woman. She tends to buy in large quantities. One woman routinely buys seven dozen pairs of stockings at once. "I simply don't have time for shopping. If I see a suit and it fits I buy it in every color," says another vice president. Adds a president, "I buy everything by the dozen. If I like a pair of shoes and they fit, I buy several of them. I never agonize over purchases. I may waste money when I shop but I don't waste time. My time is the most valuable thing I have." She does "a whole year's shopping" in about two hours. A nearby shop whose owner knows her taste and style stays open late whenever the executive wants to shop.

Most executives pick up their stockings at the grocery store when they stop by to pick up some other necessity on their way home from the office. Even with a housekeeper, trips to the grocery store seem inescapable. "Every time I'm in a grocery store I buy five pairs of stockings," comments one woman. "That way I never run out." She wears neutral beige stockings so she does not have to spend even a moment coordinating her stockings with her office garb.

The corporate woman has analyzed her existence and stripped it down to the bare essentials. If some aspect of her life is expendable, she matter-of-factly eliminates it.

She buys household supplies in large quantities also, reducing the number of times an item has to be purchased. She buys vats of detergent, gallons of mustard. She buys everything she can at one place—probably a large grocery store between her home and office.

THE COOKING

One executive cooks in large quantities and freezes the meals in smaller portions. "I make my soup in a huge lobster pot," she says. "I make spaghetti sauce in the same proportions. Give me a rainy Saturday and I'll cook enough to last us for at least a month." Her children defrost the food as needed. "Happiness at home is simply a good microwave oven," she adds.

The corporate woman frequently opts for a local restaurant instead of cooking dinner after a grueling day at the office, "We eat out at least three times a week," says a mother of two children. "Chinese food is cheap."

The executive woman may serve several take-out fast food meals during the week. "I serve bean sprouts on the weekend to make up for all the garbage I feed my family when I'm on the run," says a rueful corporate climber.

Cooking is one of the duties a corporate woman may have to relinquish, depending on her priorities and the number of demands on her time and energy. "I love to cook," says one. "But the only time I really can cook is when I'm on vacation."

THE CLOSET MOM

Despite the complications having a family brings, some women have found that a family adds a certain patina to their corporate image. "For dealing with the people who thought I was cold, that I had an icicle for a heart, having a baby has been an asset," notes a tough-minded New York executive. "Before my daughter they couldn't relate to me. Now that I'm a mother they figure maybe I'm not all bad."

It is only recently that corporations have grown tolerant of mothers functioning in the executive suite. Ten or twenty years ago, in most of corporate America children were the kiss of death to a working woman's future. Confides one executive who struggled to the top rungs of the corporate ladder from humble clerical beginnings: "I worked at one company at a level no woman had ever been promoted to before for three years before I had the courage to let them know I had two children at home. They knew I was divorced but they didn't know about the kids. I was terrified they would find out and not promote me. I needed to get ahead and I felt the kids would work against me."

Times have changed. Improvements have been made in male attitudes, but many corporate women are frightened that their role as mother and wife will work against them. They wisely give their families a low profile.

HIGH VERSUS LOW PROFILE

It is exceptional for the executive female to initiate conversations about her family at the office. Generally she does not call attention to its existence. She does not put pictures of her husband or children on her desk before she has carefully weighed the consequences.

In fact, she is more likely to have a picture of her pet than her husband on an office shelf. One industrial executive, whose hobby is photography, has several large color photographs of her dogs in her office. Pedigreed, expensive and elegant, they add the same kind of status to her office that thoroughbred horses bring to a male tycoon's executive arena.

"I didn't have pictures and never mentioned my daughter," says a woman who is alone in her high position in an otherwise male-dominated industry. "I realized all the guys have pictures of their families in their offices. Still, I feared I would be viewed more critically and males would be secretly watching for signs that I permitted my child to interfere with my work."

Even if she ventures a picture of her child in her office, a woman typically keeps a lower profile for her family than her male counterparts. "I never mention my son and I say as little as possible when I'm asked. I am very careful what I reveal about him."

Children are more of a liability for a woman's executive image than a husband. Husbands, while not displayed by their mates as prominently as men display their wives, are still occasionally in view. As mentioned earlier, if the husband is particularly successful, he adds prestige and power to a woman's corporate presence.

PREGNANT BUT POWERFUL

The history of pregnant women in the corporate white-collar work force is a recent one. Twenty years ago women were routinely fired when their pregnancy became apparent, on the male premise that very pregnant women were very disgusting to look at. Recalls a woman who has since made it to the top: "I was working as a secretary and I was six months pregnant. A client of my boss met me and said to him, 'How can you stand looking at THAT?' I was fired on the spot." That was twenty-four years ago.

Even fifteen years ago, women were caught in the corporate anti-pregnancy prejudice. Routinely, there were mandatory corporate maternity leave policies based on the "unsightliness" of pregnancy. Sandra Meyer was a group product manager at a huge food products company thirteen years ago when she became pregnant. As group product manager she was at the first level of high middle management—meaning she had joined the senior management family. Being the only woman, she was particularly visible. When she became pregnant she was caught in the archaic regulations regarding the unseemliness of having obviously pregnant women in the office. The corporate policy was that she should take off a minimum of three months before the birth and two months after. "I was concerned that if I was building an organization and I disappeared for five months I would dilute my effectiveness. There was no way I could stay out that long," states Ms. Meyer. She resisted leaving. Luckily for her, her male colleagues rallied behind her. "I refused to go," she recalls. However, rules were rules.

She negotiated with the company and they arrived at a compromise that entailed her resigning as a regular employee and continuing in her job as a per diem consultant—the anti-pregnancy rules did not mention anything about consultants. She continued as a consultant until the rules afffecting her as an employee expired. Executive Meyer worked until Thanksgiving eve, had the baby on Thanksgiving day, missed a week of work and returned to her job after taking off a total of five work days. The birth was a major event at the company, which had not previously promoted women to management. Thus it had never had a manager give birth before. Banners flew around the office celebrating the child's arrival and the chairman visited the young executive in the hospital.

Soon after, the company changed its policy concerning pregnancy. Ten years ago Ms. Meyer, working in an even higher position at the same company, gave birth to another child. It was treated as routinely as a cold. She took a whopping total of two weeks to recuperate before returning to the office.

In the past ten years, a period when women have surged into the work place, childbearing has become a matter-of-fact event. But while childbearing has become officially acceptable, it is still gingerly approached by savvy young executive women.

Some jobs make motherhood a virtual impossibility. Jobs requiring constant travel, seven-day work weeks, nonstop entertaining and long hours simply preclude the possibility of having any private life of any kind. Motherhood requires some, albeit minimal, private time.

If a woman has a particularly demanding job and decides to have a child, the decisions she faces require soul-searching. One young woman executive in the entertainment business opted for a less demanding position than her vice presidency at a film studio. "I wanted to be able to keep my weekends free," she explains. She moved to take a vice presidency at another company in a less frenetic side of the entertainment business.

When a woman intends to continue in her executive position after bearing a child, she may approach her pregnancy with many misgivings. "When I was pregnant I felt I had to show the guys it was not going to change me or my performance after I had a baby. So I was super cool," recalls a woman who bore a daughter three years ago.

Maintaining Power Throughout Pregnancy and Childbirth

- She works up until the last minute. "My children were polite enough to be born on Sunday," quips one woman.
- She dresses elegantly in conservative maternity dresses resembling suits.
- She is good-natured about jokes about her girth.
- She never initiates a conversation about the baby.
- She keeps any discussion of her pregnancy as brief as possible, e.g., the names picked out and the due date.
- She returns to the office within two weeks after giving birth and works short days at the office for the next month, taking papers home and working in bed several hours each day. It is important that her presence at the office appear essentially uninterrupted.

- If she takes off six weeks, she takes no more. She understands that men regard post-pregnancy time off as goof-off time.
- She talks to her office several times a day during her recuperation.
- She organizes her schedule and her activities to minimize the attention given to her pregnancy. (She does this so well that some of her colleagues believe she planned her pregnancy around her job and not vice versa.) Even handled with grace and skill, pregnancy is still somewhat awkward for the executive woman. "I felt how I handled my pregnancy would signal how I would handle motherhood, so I tried to ignore being pregnant. I was deeply concerned about my image as a professional woman," confides a New York–based executive.
- She arranges her doctor's appointments at the beginning or at the end of a work day so that minimum interference with her work is necessary.
- She uses her staff to compensate for any physical shortcoming she may experience because of her pregnancy, e.g., if she has difficulty in getting up and down from her chair, she has her secretary usher in colleagues while the executive remains seated—just as she would if she had a sprained ankle. Late in her term, she may arrange for a staff member to carry her luggage if she has to travel.

Things a Pregnant Executive Never Does

- She does not wear frilly, flowered maternity dresses to the office.
- She does not wear a dress that has an arrow printed on it pointing to "baby."
- She does not discuss "how hard John and I tried to get me pregnant."
- She does not permit her obstetrician to keep her waiting for hours. Her doctor's staff have been directed to inform her if the doctor is detained.
- She does not mention her pregnancy to people she does not know well when she speaks with them on the telephone. Since they do not see her, there is no reason to mention the baby.
- She does not gain excessive weight.
- She does not order pickles and ice cream at business lunches.

EXECUTIVE CHILDREN

Almost all male executives have children. After all, they have wives to take care of them.

About half of the executive women, who of course are wifeless, choose not to have children. Some of them did not have a chance to choose, though. Many of the women who have inched their way up the corporate ladder had children in the distant past when they were married to a corporate male and they were the wife. After divorcing, these women traditionally have been left with the children—and the need to make a living.

Executive mothers have learned to adjust by simplifying their lives. They move close to the school their children attend. They choose a school near the office so that home, school and office are within a short distance of each other. They find a doctor's office that their children can easily walk to.

Weekends are sacred times for working mothers. Fifteen-hour work days during the week are tolerable if the weekend is free to spend with the children.

The children are sent to school at as young an age as possible and taught at an early age to be self-reliant. "They started cleaning their own rooms from the time they could walk. As soon as they could reach the table they were helping with breakfast. When they were ten they learned to do their own laundry," states an executive whose work experience began on the bottom rung of corporate life after her marriage ended.

The children of these hardworking women seem to adapt easily. When they play "house," office is part of their perception. The little girl of a working mother likely enacts leaving for and arriving from the office as part of her game of "house." When she is playing her games the daughter of an absent mother makes mock phone calls, instructing the home person to defrost the hamburger and take the clothes out of the dryer.

Mornings are the most hectic time in the life of a working mother. Organizing the children's clothes for the day, getting them dressed and preparing breakfast while throwing together her own executive look is a tough task. "Some mornings I think we're just not going to make it that day," confesses one executive. "But the kids are terrific. They help as much as they can."

"The biggest fear of a working mother is whether the children will develop the right values when you aren't there with them all day every day. That really worried me the most," confides a woman whose children, incidentally, turned out wonderfully by all objective standards.

Working mothers concentrate on doing the personal things for their child. They do the nighttime and morning feedings for their infants. They dress the baby in the mornings.

After a tough day in the corporate corridors, an executive mother can find herself drained and ill-equipped to deal with the demands of their families. But these overachieving women somehow rise to the occasion. "There are nights when I go home and as I approach the house and look at the lights I think that the kids are going to be irritable, tired and hungry and I think 'I can't go in there. I'm too tired.' But of course I go in and the kids clamor for attention and I am filled with guilt," says one executive mother. She draws on her reserve energy and helps her children with their homework, discusses their problems and reads them a bed time story before she finally gets a chance to rest herself.

The busy managerial woman uses the same skills she uses in directing the efforts of people who report to her to manage her home. Lists are the essence of her existence and the telephone becomes the pipeline between the office and home as routinely as it is between Chicago and Houston.

The children report in when they come home from school and ask permission to leave the premises. The mother gives them instructions about dinner preparation and her schedule each day. If she is busy in meetings she has her staff prepared to do this for her.

When a child is injured in school, the teacher calls the mother at her office. If the child can walk to the doctor, the executive phones the doctor's office. When the child has been checked, the doctor phones the mother and reports.

The executive woman is constantly evaluating the problems of her children, weighing her priorities of motherhood against corporatehood. If the child has a scratch and she has a meeting with the president, she goes to the meeting with the president. If the child has a broken leg and she has a staff meeting, she postpones the staff meeting.

Having a husband can be helpful when it comes to dealing with a sick child. "The one who is more available leaps into action. My husband has a less structured job. He can more easily go home," observes one vice president.

If a child requires regular medical care, the executive woman arranges to take vacation time as illness necessitates. She constantly evaluates how her involvement with her family is going to be perceived by her co-workers and superiors. Under no circumstances does she permit her image as a mother to undermine her image as a corporate manager.

If a child has chicken pox or the mumps, she arranges for a babysitter and checks in by phone throughout the day or has a staff member monitor the situation. Once again, the telephone is her instrument for reassuring the child of her interest while permitting her to continue functioning in her office.

She probably has a problem with restricting the phone calls the children make to her. "I'd get a call from my daughter saying, 'Mom, Johnny is pulling my pigtails.' Then I'd get a call from Johnny saying, 'Sally won't let me use the Betamax,' " admits one executive. "It's tough because you want them to know you care but you don't want them to bother you. You have to set rules and guidelines and punishment/reward systems related to them."

Sometimes the phone calls can be embarrassing. One executive mother was with a client at a restaurant when the maître d' asked her if she would take a phone call at the table. She agreed, thinking her office was trying to reach her. Instead, she was connected to her hysterical nine-year-old daughter, who had not been picked up at a distant airport by her grandmother due to a mixup. Dealing with the terrified daughter without letting the client discover it was not a business call was very difficult. "That was a very interesting conversation from his point of view, I'm sure," recalls the woman. She has a solution for that kind of dilemma: "I have never accepted a phone call at a restaurant table since." She simply leaves the table to take the call.

In short, the corporate mother manages all the aspects of her complex existence without calling attention to aspects of her life outside of the office. She makes a complicated life appear simple.

Since she is competing with men in a man's world, she calls no attention to her fundamental liability—the lack of a wife at home.

EXECUTIVE MARRIAGE

Recent studies indicate that executive women are about equally divided between the camp of "I do" and the camp of "I don't." About half of them have chosen to be married while the other half chose to be unmarried. (If an executive is divorced, she doesn't refer to herself as divorced. She prefers "unmarried"—the word tells less about her personal history. "Divorcee" is a word still laden with fallen-women connotations.)

The executive woman who understands that she adds another role to her role as office overachiever when she takes—or keeps—a husband has few illusions. "Let's face it. Being married takes valuable time and energy," observes one woman at the top.

RELATED VERSUS UNRELATED FIELDS

"Life would be simpler if I were single. But it probably wouldn't be as interesting. A husband is one more responsibility to juggle," notes a senior executive at an industrial company, whose husband conducts medical research. She has found that having a mate in a field totally removed from hers lends another dimension to her life. His problems have no resemblance to hers. They bring a fresh perspective to each other. "When I tell him about the office it's like describing life on another planet to him," she says.

Marriage to someone in an unrelated field expands a woman's world and can bring insights that freshen her perspective.

Other women have found a different advantage in being married—the proverbial pillow talk can be very constructive. They married men who work in similar businesses facing similar problems. Being married to a man in a related field provides a much-needed sounding board, notes a woman in the food service business who married one of her company's suppliers. "He is my confidant. Our communicating about business helps make the marriage work."

IT CAN BE A PLUS

"Work can be such a consuming mistress you lose track of the need to grow in outside areas. Women are prone to be married to their jobs and not be well-rounded. Children and husbands force you to have something in your life besides your work," states Colombe Nicholas.

Having a husband makes it easier for a woman to admit who goes along with her to the country or to the south of France on vacation. Says one woman who married for eminently practical reasons, "Finally I can level about who goes places with me. For years when I was unmarried I always had to answer, 'Friends.' Getting married was a way to get my man out of the closet."

Many women have indeed found marriage a practical arrangement. Since most male executives are married, some women feel that having a husband makes them appear more acceptable to their male peers. Some men who find it difficult to deal with the woman executive may find it much more comfortable to talk with her husband. Thus an executive's husband can play an important role as a social buffer—something executives' wives have done for a century.

"I hate to admit it, but that "Mrs." makes me look more respectable. I wish it were not that way and I know it shouldn't be that way, but it's a fact. Being married legitimizes me in the eyes of most of my co-workers," notes a woman.

Marriage provides a social insulation. "Marriage allows me to avoid sexual advances. It gives me an easy out," opines an attractive young executive. "I can slide away from any sexual overtones by the mere mention of my husband's name. It works like a charm."

Marriage is an important emotional support system for some women, one they find delivers much more to their lives than it takes away.

A supportive husband can be a strong ally. "There are lots of people out there telling you everything you do wrong, telling you that you can't do something. My husband tells me how good I am, how good I can be," notes a broadcast executive.

MAKING IT WORK

The corporate woman's husband has to be a special breed. For one thing, he has to be flexible. This means there are nights when he fixes his own dinner or eats out while his wife takes clients to dinner. There are nights when he cooks for the two of them. There are other nights when she is required to attend industry-related dinners. The corporate husband usually chooses to stay home and recuperate from his day at his office. "We don't go to each other's trade dinners unless we have to," says one busy sales executive. She is married to a man who is president of a firm in an unrelated business. She confides: "Michael recently ordered two boxes of leftover World War II K-rations. I think that's a hint he'd like for me to cook dinner more often, but I ignored it. I just phone up and say, 'Fix yourself a K-ration, darling. I don't know when I'll be able to come home.' "

The marriage works better if the corporate husband is also preoccupied with his work. "Husbands of executives are people who also need their space and understand why their wives need space. The husband needs to do his own thing," notes Colombe Nicholas.

"Our marriage is perfect," observes a professional woman married to an executive man. "We're both workaholics." Shared time in the two-career marriage is frequently limited to spending as much of the weekend as possible together and taking vacations together.

Corporate women find it necessary to apply guidelines to their marriages in order to preserve shared time. For instance, one couple has a rule that Sundays are sacred—they both plan to leave Sunday completely free and spend it together. They tend also to take frequent trips together or withdraw to a quiet country house together. "Airplanes are where we do most of our talking," comments a peripatetic executive. The logistics of coordinating schedules can be complex. "Our secretaries talk to each other every day," says a corporate woman.

With planning—careful planning and scheduling are essential in every aspect of executive life—couples can arrange somewhat parallel existences.

The ideal executive marriage is between two successful people both toiling diligently at rewarding careers and savoring their brief times together.

WHEN TWO CAREERS DON'T KEEP PACE

Problems arise if the husband's success does not keep pace with the corporate woman's. Men, adrift with no role model, tend to feel humiliated when their wives outpace them. "My husband is in an unrelated field working at another company. But there is a point at which it has become impossible to ignore my greater success," confides a senior vice president of a prestigious multinational corporation. Not only does she make more money than her husband; she works for a more important company. She also has certain other perks that rub salt in his wounded pride—the limousine, the use of a private jet, the entourage of assistants, the unstinted expense account. In the current American society, these trappings have traditionally been male. Only an exceptional husband can cope with the fact that his wife earned them while he did not.

Moreover, when the wife outpaces her husband, he ceases to be a social asset for her in her corporate life. The corporate peers of the executive woman are conditioned to seek out men as successful as or more successful than they are.

The woman who opts for marriage does not expect it to simplify her life. If her husband is over 40 years old she understands that he is likely to be a mixed luxury. Men in that age group have frequently been conditioned by their mothers—who probably never worked outside of the home—to expect the women they marry to assume complete responsibility for the household. No matter how much these men love and care for their working wives they are unlikely to assume a fair share of the responsibility for the family's domestic life. They probably don't even know how.

The executive woman understands that her son is far more likely to be a full partner in *his* family when he grows up because he has a mother (her) who works outside of the home and has been a very different role model than his grandmother (his father's mother).

Just as she often has to educate the men she deals with at the office, the successful woman is frequently an educator at home. Once again her patience, good humor, and resourcefulness are called into play. She builds a support system that makes it possible for her to manage her husband's personal life, as well as her own, knowing that, in time, her mate will probably assume more and more of the responsibility. She understands that for the time being only one member of the marriage is likely to be in fact a "helpmate"—her. "How do my husband and I divide the chores?" comments a hard-driving executive woman. "We don't. Basically I do most of them."

EXECUTIVE COMPROMISES

The achieving corporate woman has been forced to conclude that she must choose what things are most important to her. She has to let other things slide. "I'm trying to juggle my family and my job and to be good at both. But I can't do everything all of the time," says an entertainment executive. She gave up "a tidy house, going to the store whenever I like, and looking great every day."

The "tidy house" is one of the first things let go after a woman pares her life down to its bare essentials. "I could not spend time with the children, work fifteen hours a day, run our lives and have a clean house too," reflects a single parent.

Other choices must be faced. One woman who valued personal space says "I was able to go to my own part of the house where it was quiet and orderly and calm. I could unwind there away from the children." Being able to afford a spacious house required her to move to an unfashionable part of town where real estate was inexpensive. "The personal space meant more than the neighborhood," she avers.

Those choices are not made without careful thought. As one top woman executive says, "I never tried to be superwoman. Still I don't think there is a woman in the world that doesn't feel inadequate. Something has to give somewhere." Deciding what gives is never easy.

What an executive ultimately ends up sacrificing is part of herself. With all the demands that fall on her shoulders and without a wife at home to rely on, the corporate woman carves the additional time to nurture herself out of what would have been time spent resting or vacationing. She has no time for leisure reading. No time for the facialist or manicurist. No time for goofing off. No time to visit with friends or go out on nonbusiness dates.

"The hardest adjustment is having no time for myself at all," admits an married executive who has a young child. "I'd love to just have fifteen minutes to read a leisure magazine," she adds dreamily.

"What I would like more than anything—more than a raise or a bonus—would be the privilege of going to exercise class at three in the afternoon," confides a woman who loathes getting up at six in the morning. "Exercising in the morning before the sun even comes up is a bummer. But that's the only time I have for myself—sleep time." She does not delude herself. "I chose to be married and to work and to have the baby. I almost have it all. I could if there were just more hours in the day."

Personal days off from the office are likely spent taking the baby to the specialist, getting a haircut, buying clothes and getting a pedicure. Excitement is not what successful women with families seek in their time off from the office—unless sleep is exciting. Vacation time becomes sleep time at a quiet retreat or a soothing week at a health spa.

One New York woman takes a vacation week to stay at her apartment and enjoy the Big Apple. "My apartment is beautiful. But I spend so much time working to afford it I don't have time to enjoy it. Other people spend money to come to Manhattan for their vacations," she continues. "I'm usually too busy to take advantage of living here. So I spend a week here on vacation." To assure that she is not interrupted by her office, everyone except one senior staff member is told she is spending the week in London. Otherwise she would be too accessible. "If they think I'm far away, they handle problems without me," she says. During that week she indulges herself: She goes to museums, has a facial every day, goes to exercise class for an extra hour every day. "I take the money I would spend on transportation and accommodations somewhere else and spend it all on spoiling myself. It's great. I return to work after a week really feeling like you're supposed to feel after a wonderful vacation."

Some companies are more understanding than others of the enormous total life demands faced by the executive woman. Frequently, companies headed by younger men are more understanding of the multiple roles a woman juggles. Says an executive married mother, "I'm lucky. The president of my company appreciates what his full-time wife does for him. He keeps reminding me that he knows I don't have a wife." Her president is forty years old.

When managers are over sixty years old, they are of a generation that has little understanding of today's successful working woman. "They think, 'Why isn't she home taking care of the baby?' " notes an industrial vice president.

Upon reflection, the executive may consider alternatives to her life-style such as "dropping out" or opting for a more traditional housewife role. She may even have some regrets about the sacrifices her complex life requires. But she cannot imagine living any other way. One executive, a mother in her mid-thirties, admits she would be reluctant to stay home and be a full-time wife and mother. "I'm at the point now where I'm caught. I am damned if I do and damned if I don't. I would miss the sense of self-worth I get from my job. I would miss the social reinforcement and the power. I'm torn. It's important to know that I can rely on myself and that I'm really good at something.

"Making money is important," she continues. "The power of having money is more important than I had realized when I didn't have it."

The ego reinforcement provided by success in the business world offsets the juggling act an executive woman has to perform to manage all the aspects of her life. "The power is a thrill. I see the effect I have on people when I come into a meeting. I get a constant reaffirmation similar to the kind that a movie star gets," declares a very successful thirty-six-year-old woman.

In the end, the money and power offset the pain.

INDEX